How Schools Are
Killing Reading
and What You
Can Do About It

Readicide

Kelly Gallagher

Foreword by Richard Allington

Stenhouse Publishers
Portland, Maine

Stenhouse Publishers
www.stenhouse.com

Credits
Page 8: Testing cartoon © 2007 *The Record*, reprinted by permission of Jimmy Margulies.
Page 33: Bridge to Prison cartoon © 2008 Bob Englehart. Reprinted with permission.
Page 70: "Introduction to Poetry," from *The Apple That Astonished Paris* by Billy Collins. Copyright © 1988, 1996 Billy Collins. Reprinted with permission of the University of Arkansas Press.

Library of Congress Cataloging-in-Publication Data
Gallagher, Kelly, 1958-
    Readicide : how schools are killing reading and what you can do about it / Kelly Gallagher.
        p. cm.
    Includes bibliographical references.
    ISBN 978-1-57110-780-0 (alk. paper)
    1. Reading—United States. 2. Literacy—United States. 3. Reading promotion—United States. I. Title.
    LB1050.G25 2009
    428.4—dc22

                                                                2008040694

Cover, interior design, and typesetting by Martha Drury

Manufactured in the United States of America on acid-free, recycled paper
15 14 13 12 11 10 09   9 8 7 6 5 4 3

For those educators who resist

the political in favor of the authentic

con•tents

fore•word

Readicide by Kelly Gallagher is one of those few must-read books that appear every year in education. Although the primary focus of the book is on adolescents' reading, or the lack of it, the message is one that will ring true for teachers of grades K–12.

Gallagher defines *readicide* early on as "the systematic killing of the love of reading, often exacerbated by the inane, mind-numbing practices found in schools." He then documents just how widely readicide is practiced and discusses its outcomes. Citing recent reports from the National Endowment for the Humanities and the National Assessment of Educational Progress, he illustrates how powerful readicide has been in creating *aliterates*—people who can read but largely do not.

The data available indicate that we are producing more and more aliterates every year. In many cases, we do so with good intentions. State and national initiatives linked to the No Child Left Behind (NCLB) Act of 2001 have created schools in which lessons are focused primarily on improving reading test scores. As a result, instruction has been narrowed and made even more mind-numbing than in earlier eras (and those eras did not provide much to celebrate). The end result is that evaluations of the effects of NCLB have demonstrated no improvement in actual reading achievement[1] and instead show a disturbing potential for fostering readicide.

---

1. Gamse, B. C., R. T. Jacob, M. Horst, B. Boulay, and F. Unlu. 2008. *Reading First Impact Study Final Report* (Report No. NCEE 2009-4038). Washington, DC: National Center for Education Evaluation and Regional Assistance, Institute of Education Sciences, U.S. Department of Education.

As a classroom teacher, Gallagher understands the readicide pressures that teachers face and, in this book, offers a solution. He provides readers with a hopeful alternative—one that not only fulfills state standards but also meets his central standard of creating literate and productive citizens.

As a researcher, I visit classrooms to observe instruction. Gallagher isn't a researcher in the traditional sense, but his examination can open the eyes of many researchers and help to improve current and future work in this area. Yet this book remains, primarily, a book for teachers. It is a relatively brief text—one that can be read in a weekend (without spending the entire weekend reading it). It is also a book written with the soul of a teacher at its heart. If every middle and high school teacher would read this book and act on the recommendations it offers, I'd worry less about my grandchildren's education.

Richard L. Allington
University of Tennessee

ac•knowl•edg•ments

Big-time thanks to the following:

My wife, Kristin, for her extraordinary support. Through the course of writing this book, she has been my travel agent, airport courier, luggage tracker, researcher, website editor, problem solver, FedEx-er, sounding board, and psychologist. There is no one better to have on your side when O'Hare is evacuated at 1:00 a.m.

Caitlin and Devin—always. I could not be prouder.

My mom and dad, who made sure I stayed off the road to readicide.

Bill Varner, my editor at Stenhouse, who has not only worked hard to shape all four of my books but also has always been extra gracious every time the Red Sox eliminate the Angels in the playoffs. Bill's adept touch is found throughout these pages.

Chris Downey and Jay Kilburn, for their dedicated work on the design and production of this book, and to Nate Butler, who in the course of wearing many hats at Stenhouse makes my life easier. Thanks also to Andre Barnett, whose keen copyediting eye makes me look smarter than I am, and to Martha Drury, who designed yet another great cover.

Richard Allington, for his years of dedication in promoting authentic reading instruction for our nation's children.

My students at Magnolia High School in Anaheim, California, who provided the inspiration for this book.

My friends and colleagues in the English Department at MHS: Amie Howell, Melissa Hunnicutt, Virginia Kim, Katrina Mundy, Esther Noh, Kallie Pappas, Sherri Rothwell, Lindsay Ruben, Sara Steiner, Margaret Tagler, Robin Turner, Sarah Valenzuela, Michelle Waxman, and Dana White. Amazing how a baked potato can raise the spirits of an entire department, isn't it?

Steve Gonzales, for your continued dedication to the students of Magnolia High School.

Dr. Denise Selbe, my new principal, for all she does to support literacy at MHS.

John Chapman, for reasons only he knows.

Debbie Miller, who, when I complained that I no longer had time to write, said, "Just try to write fifteen minutes every day." She has no idea how helpful that advice was and is.

Smokey Daniels, the King of the Hampton Inn, who coined the term "readicide" when we had lunch together in (fill in name of the restaurant) in (fill in name of the city) in (fill in name of the state).

Chris Crutcher, for introducing me to Basheeba. I am forever grateful, especially when driving the back roads of Oklahoma at 6:30 a.m.

Jeff Anderson, because . . . well . . . just because.

And last, my dog, Beezus, who lay faithfully at my feet each day as I tried to write coherent sentences at the ungodly hour of 4:00 a.m., when most of this book, without coffee, was written.

in•tro•duc•tion

Learning without thinking is labor lost; thinking without learning is dangerous.

—Confucius

Every year, those who publish dictionaries are faced with a central question: which emerging words should be added to the new editions? Because some words have longer life expectancies than others, these decisions are not taken lightly. To make it into a dictionary, a new word must not only show evidence that it has been around a few years but also that it demonstrates some indication of staying power. With these criteria in mind, the editors at Merriam-Webster have chosen a number of new entries for the *Merriam-Webster's Collegiate Dictionary*, eleventh edition (2006). Recognizing that new words can tell us a bit about our culture, here are five of my favorites:

drama queen: noun, a person given to often excessively emotional performances or reactions

gastric bypass: noun, a surgical bypass operation that typically involves reducing the size of the stomach and reconnecting the smaller stomach to bypass the first portion of the small intestine so as to restrict food intake and reduce caloric absorption in cases of severe obesity

mouse potato: noun, a person who spends a great deal of time using a computer

soul patch: noun, a small growth of beard under a man's lower lip

supersize: transitive verb, to increase considerably the size, amount, or extent of

With all due respect to the folks at Merriam-Webster, I begin this book by proposing a new word for their next edition. To make it easy on the editors, I also include its definition:

> **Read-i-cide:** noun, the systematic killing of the love of reading, often exacerbated by the inane, mind-numbing practices found in schools

Recognizing that this new word and its definition are potentially offensive, I did not arrive at the definition of readicide lightly. The coinage of this word emerges from my twenty-two years as a classroom teacher, from my work as a district-level language arts coordinator, and from my travels around this country as a literacy consultant. I introduce "readicide" here because it cuts to the central ironic thesis of this book: rather than helping students, many of the reading practices found in today's classrooms are actually contributing to the death of reading. In an earnest attempt to instill reading, teachers and administrators push practices that kill many students' last chance to develop into lifelong readers.

The Onset of Readicide

Because the powers outside the classroom walls are so strong in tearing down young readers, what goes on inside the classroom is of paramount importance. Today, more than ever, valuable classroom time presents the best opportunity—often the only opportunity—to turn kids on to reading. Unfortunately, this isn't occurring. Consider the following points taken from *NCTE Principles of Adolescent Literacy Reform* (2006), a publication from the National Council of Teachers of English:

* The National Assessment of Educational Progress shows that secondary school students are reading significantly below expected levels.
* The National Assessment of Adult Literacy finds that literacy scores of high school graduates dropped between 1992 and 2003.

✖ The Alliance for Excellent Education points to 8.7 million secondary students—that is one in four—who are unable to read and comprehend the material in textbooks.

✖ The National Center for Education Statistics reports a continuous and significant reading achievement gap between racial/ethnic/economic groups.

✖ Three thousand students with limited literacy skills drop out of school every day in this country.

✖ The 2005 ACT College Readiness Benchmark for Reading found that only about half the students tested were ready for college-level reading, and the 2005 scores were the lowest in the decade.

✖ The American Institutes for Research reports that only 13 percent of American adults are capable of performing complex literacy tasks.

These findings point to further trouble. Another recent study, *Reading at Risk*, found that only 16 percent of adults are "frequent" or "avid" readers of literary text:

Adult Reading Frequency of Literary Texts

Reading Frequency	Percentage Who Read
Nonliterary readers	54%
Light readers	21%
Moderate readers	9%
Frequent readers	12%
Avid readers	4%

Source: National Endowment for the Arts, *Reading at Risk* (2004).

In addition, *USA Today* reported that 27 percent of adults in this country did not read a single book in 2007 (Toppo 2007).

You do not need to read study after study to sense the degree of readicide in schools today. Instead, talk to any kindergarten teacher. Ask her about students' attitudes in her classroom during reading time, and it is likely she will tell you about her students' enthusiasm. Then, ask a fifth-grade teacher the same question. You'll likely receive a mixed response. Finish your field research by again asking a twelfth-grade teacher the same question, and note his quick exasperation (be prepared to measure the emergence of this exasperation in nanoseconds). This unfortunate shifting of reading attitudes—from enthusiasm to indifference to hostility—is a pattern I have witnessed firsthand during numerous visits to schools across this country. But I don't need to visit other schools to see this; I witness it firsthand in my own classroom. Consider these comments from some of my 2007–8 students when I asked them during the first week of school to share anonymously their thoughts about reading:

"Reading, I hate it because of the lack of fun it brings me."

"I never really liked reading, but I don't have many books."

"Reading is only fun if I have nothing else to do."

"Hate runs through me when I spend hours of time I could be spending doing something enjoyable."

"Reading! I find it boring—it just has no interest for me."

"Reading is a big waste of time."

"Reading really sucks."

"I read books only because my teachers make me."

"I would rather watch TV, play sports, and hang out with my friends."

To be fair, I have a smattering of students who enjoy reading, but there are fewer of them. The number of readers dwindles with each passing year.

Looking Beyond the Usual Suspects

As teachers consider the decline of reading, most point to the usual suspects—poverty, lack of parental education, print-poor environments at home, second-language issues, the era of the hurried child, and other (and easier) entertainment options that lure students away from reading. Certainly, these are all legitimate factors when examining the decline of reading, and it is not the intention of this book to minimize them. Indeed, as a teacher in an urban high school, I struggle against these factors each day in my classroom. They are real, and they impede my ability to develop young readers. But despite these real-world obstacles, I have walked into my classroom each year convinced I could turn many of my reluctant readers around. Why have I remained optimistic? Because school is where I have the opportunity to discuss books with my students. At school, students are given both time and a place to read interesting books. And at school, educators are more interested in developing lifelong readers than in developing short-term test-takers.

Unfortunately, I can no longer say with any confidence that this is the case in many classrooms. The focus has changed in our schools and not in a good way. High-interest reading is being squeezed out in favor of more test preparation practice. Interesting books are disappearing as funding is diverted to purchase "magic pill" reading programs. Sustained silent reading time is being abandoned because it is often seen as "soft" or "nonacademic." For many students, academic reading, though incredibly important, has become their only reading. (How would you like it if the *only* reading you ever did in your life was Shakespeare and *Beowulf*?) To make matters worse, students are drowning in marginalia and a sea of sticky notes. When you add all of these school practices to the forces working against readers outside the classroom, is it any surprise that mass readicide is occurring?

The purpose of this book is not to question the good intentions of well-meaning educators. I can't think of a nobler cause than teachers who spend their lives dedicated to improving their students' literacy. But isn't it disconcerting to recognize that despite massive efforts, massive amounts of money spent, and massive attention to the decline of reading, we are still losing large numbers of young readers? I have witnessed this pattern in too many schools, in too many states, to draw any conclusion other than a painful one: that the practices we, as educators, are employing to make students better readers are often killing them. Intentions are not the problem; our practices are the problem.

As teachers of adolescents, we must take a hard look at what we are doing to potential readers. After thirteen years of schooling, many graduates are thankful they may never have to open another book again. A generation of readers is being lost, and it is time for teachers to consider how and why our practices may be contributing to this decline in reading. When I asked one of my students about reading, she wrote, "I am not really interested in books, pages, and words." Imagine a student who graduates from high school uninterested in books, pages, and words.

What factors inside our high schools would lead a senior to declare she is not really interested in books, pages, and words? What is causing readicide? I suggest there are four major contributing factors:

✖ Schools value the development of test-takers more than they value the development of readers
✖ Schools are limiting authentic reading experiences
✖ Teachers are overteaching books
✖ Teachers are underteaching books

These factors form the focus of the chapters that follow. Each chapter will take an in-depth look at one of these causes of readicide. More important, each chapter will end by exploring what we can do to avoid graduating students who have no interest in books, pages, and words.

Ray Bradbury said, "You don't have to burn books to destroy culture. Just get people to stop reading them." With that dire warning in mind, let's begin examining what we can do to stem the tide of readicide.

The Elephant in the Room

When we consider what to do about readicide, we must start with the elephant in the room: how the overemphasis on testing is playing a major part in killing off readers in America's classrooms. This is ironic because the mission statement or the desired educational outcomes of most schools in this country highly value reading. What do teachers and curriculum directors mean by "value" reading? A look at the practices of most schools suggests that when a school "values" reading, what it really means is that the school intensely focuses on raising state-mandated reading test scores—the kind of reading our students will rarely, if ever, do in adulthood. "Valuing reading" is often a euphemism for preparing students to pass mandated multiple-choice exams, and in dragging students down this path, schools are largely contributing to the development of readicide. Sadly, in overemphasizing reading that students will confront on standardized reading tests, schools are working against developing independent readers.

I am not against teaching students how to take a test. Indeed, we want all of our students to have test-taking knowledge. However, the overemphasis of teaching reading through the lens of preparing students for state-mandated reading tests has become so completely unbalanced that it is drowning any chance our adolescents have of developing into lifelong readers. We are developing test-takers at the expense of readers.

Jimmy Margulies
The Record (Hackensack, N.J.)
King Features Syndicate

The emphasis on test preparation harms young readers in two ways:

Reason 1: A curriculum steeped in multiple-choice test preparation drives shallow teaching and learning.

Reason 2: Rather than lift up struggling readers, an emphasis on multiple-choice test preparation ensures that struggling readers will continue to struggle. Test preparation reading plays a large part in maintaining "apartheid schools."

Let's take a moment to examine each reason in detail.

Reason I: A Curriculum Steeped in Multiple-Choice Test Preparation Drives Shallow Teaching and Learning

To prepare students for the state test in tenth-grade social studies, teachers in my state are responsible for a staggering amount of content. In one school year, sophomores are expected

✖ to relate the moral and ethical principles in ancient Greek and Roman philosophy, in Judaism, and in Christianity to the development of Western political thought;

✖ to compare and contrast the Glorious Revolution of England, the American Revolution, and the French Revolution and their enduring effects worldwide on the political expectations for self-government and individual liberty;

✖ to analyze the effects of the Industrial Revolution in England, France, Germany, Japan, and the United States;

✖ to analyze patterns of global change in the era of New Imperialism in at least two of the following regions or countries: Africa, Southeast Asia, China, India, Latin America, and the Philippines;

✖ to analyze the causes and course of World War I;

✖ to analyze the effects of World War I;

✖ to analyze the rise of totalitarian governments after World War I;

✖ to analyze the causes and consequences of World War II;

✖ to analyze the international developments in the post–World World War II world;

✖ to analyze instances of nation-building in the contemporary world in at least two of the following regions or countries: the Middle East, Africa, Mexico and other parts of Latin America, and China;

✖ to analyze the integration of countries into the world economy and the information, technological, and communications revolutions (e.g., television, satellites, computers).

I am not against these standards. Standards are critical in helping teachers plan and align their instruction. If the powers-that-be took away every mandated test tomorrow, I would still want to know the state's definition of good teaching. I would continue to read the standards carefully, with an eye for preparing meaningful lessons for my students. Standards are necessary, and having them has made me a better teacher. However, there is one big problem concerning the state and local standards in this country: there are too many of them. Is it just me, or would it take weeks to teach any one of the preceding standards with any depth?

Officially, I am not a social studies teacher, but a state standard requires that my twelfth-grade English students write historical research papers. Last year, the topic was 9/11, and it took six weeks of teaching before my students understood the historical underpinnings and significance of that single day in history. If it took six weeks of heavy teaching before my students deeply understood the events of 9/11, then how long will it take to teach students in a history class to "relate the moral and ethical principles in ancient Greek and Roman philosophy, in Judaism, and in Christianity to the development of Western political thought"? And that's just one of many standards for which tenth-grade history teachers are responsible.

Being "held responsible" really means one thing to classroom teachers—teaching to the state- and federally mandated exams administered each spring. (Teachers do not even get the entire school year before being held accountable.) Knowing that the tests are coming in the spring and that they will cover an impossible amount of standards thrusts teachers into an unwinnable situation: either they teach all standards shallowly to make sure the content on the test is covered before students sit down to take the exams, or they slow down and teach deeply, thus sacrificing their test scores by not covering all the content that will be on the exam. With sanctions and economic penalties dangling overhead, job evaluations hanging in the balance, and results of each school's performance printed in the newspaper for the community to see, is it any wonder which path most teachers take?

A Double Whammy

Of course, the biggest danger of sprinting through various readings in any content area is that we graduate students who do not develop an interest in any content area. Authentic interest is generated when students are given the opportunity to delve deeply into an interesting idea. I am reminded why I learned so little history in high school—my teachers sprinted to cover the curriculum. Unfortunately, a course a mile wide and an inch deep might help raise test scores, but, in the process, real learning is often sacrificed. Worse, a double whammy is created: by sacrificing deep, rich teaching, we begin chipping away at our students' motivation. Want to extinguish an adolescent's curiosity? Cover as much material as possible.

There is a big difference between memorizing facts and understanding history, between teachers simply being information dispensers versus teachers turning students into deep thinkers. Unfortunately, I was exposed to the sprint-through-the-book philosophy, and as a result, it was nearly twenty years after high school before I started reading history again. I fear many of my students, in this rush to cover all material for the spring tests, will leave our schools uninterested in history, in science, in literature, and in reading.

In *Many Children Left Behind* (Meier et al. 2004), a number of examples are given to illustrate how testing has driven shallow teaching and learning:

✖ The New York City history teacher who in a sprint to cover material that might be found on the state test had one stretch in which he taught the scientific revolution, French Revolution, revolution in Haiti, Simon Bolivar and Latin American independence movements, the Napoleonic period, nineteenth-century nationalism in Italy and Germany, Zionism, and back to the Industrial Revolution (Meier et al. 2004, 40).

✖ Bruce Alberts, president of the National Academy of Sciences, notes that as children progress through elementary school, science classes are "reduced to memorizing thirty different kinds of whales and spitting out that information." Alberts points to standardized testing as the culprit, adding that "it's easier to test for facts than [for] understanding" (Meier et al. 2004, 41).

✖ In many Philadelphia schools, "students are reading fewer books to make more room for test prep" (Meier et al. 2004, 57). From California to New York, I have been approached by numerous teachers who have told me that in this drive to raise test scores, they are no longer allowed to teach novels. In an attempt to raise reading scores, school districts across the country *are removing books* from kids.

✖ The curriculum is being narrowed to make more room for test preparation. For example, "Baltimore schools are spending 20 percent less time on social studies, one of the many subjects not on the state-mandated tests and therefore receiving less attention and fewer resources. Oregon is cutting foreign language and music classes and spending more on data collection and testing programs" (Meier et al. 2004, 57).

In an analysis of the standards found in a typical K–12 school system, Robert J. Marzano found that "the knowledge and skills these documents describe represent about 3,500 benchmarks. To cover all this content, you would have to change schooling from K–12 to K–22" (Marzano and Kendall 1998, 5). Marzano's findings raise a central point: when teachers try to cram twenty-two years of curriculum into a K–12 time frame, everyone loses. The teachers are forced to adopt a shallow approach, sprinting through material. Students develop into memorizers instead of into thinkers. And both teachers' and students' motivation are irreparably harmed. Marzano's conclusion is even more telling: "By my reckoning we would have to cut content by about two-thirds. *The sheer number of standards is the biggest impediment to implementing standards*" (5; my emphasis).

Reason 2: Rather Than Lift Up Struggling Readers, an Emphasis on Multiple-Choice Test Preparation Ensures That Struggling Readers Will Continue to Struggle. Test Preparation Reading Plays a Large Part in Maintaining "Apartheid Schools."

Teachers often complain about "teaching to the test," but teaching to the test is a good thing if the test is a good test. I always teach to a test. For example, before my students reach Chapter 1 in any novel, I determine what the final exam essay question will be. What's more, I give my students the final exam question before we begin reading the novel. When the finish line is predetermined, I am a better teacher and my students are more focused readers. Teaching to the test is the foundation of good teaching, and when every minute counts, teaching to the test provides necessary focus, so time is not wasted.

Teaching to the test is not the problem. The problem occurs when we spend most of our time teaching to a shallow test. To illustrate this point, let's look at two test questions. Both ask students to consider the author's theme. Test question A is an actual question on the California High School Exit Exam. Test question B is one I have written and use in my classroom:

Test Question A*	Test Question B
Which of the following themes is developed in the article: A. the conflict between art and science B. the importance of technology C. the joy of exploration D. the difficulty of being true to oneself	Identify Golding's central theme in *Lord of the Flies* and analyze how this theme is developed through the author's use of symbolism. Cite specific examples from the text, making sure you move beyond simply summarizing.

*http://www.cde.ca.gov/ta/tg/hs/resources.asp.

I am not arguing for the elimination of all multiple-choice exams. On the contrary, teaching students how to take these tests (test question A) provides them skills they will use as they progress through school and beyond. Multiple-choice exams are not the problem; the out-of-control, overemphasized, all-consuming teaching to these standardized tests has become the problem.

Forget for a moment that the four choices for test question A are not really themes (a true theme is expressed in a complete thought; these answers are simply topics) and ask yourself: What do these two test questions value?

What Does Question A Value?	What Does Question B Value?
✖ Understanding "theme" ✖ The ability to revisit the text and *recognize* the theme ✖ Test taking skills (e.g., eliminating answers) ✖ Intelligent guessing	✖ Understanding "theme" ✖ The ability to revisit the text and *create* a theme ✖ Deep analysis of a major literary work (recognizing and analyzing both theme and symbolism) ✖ Synthesis of ideas ✖ The ability to organize thoughts into an essay, which includes having a clear thesis statement, effective transitions, developed commentary, and a conclusion

Which one produces the level of thinking I want my students to achieve? In which classroom, one that emphasizes test question A or one that emphasizes test question B, would you want your own children to be enrolled?

Another problem with a curriculum that depends heavily on students focusing on acquiring facts is that facts change. Robert J. Sternberg (2007/2008), former president of the American Psychological Association and current dean of the School of Arts and Sciences at Tufts University, notes that the "facts" he learned years ago in his introductory psychology course matter little today. "An introductory course today," he says, "contains almost entirely different facts." Instead of pounding factoids into our students' heads, Sternberg suggests that we should be emphasizing those skills that would make our students "expert citizens": "creativity, common sense, wisdom, ethics, dedication, honesty, teamwork, hard work, knowing how to win and how to lose, a sense of fair play, and lifelong learning. *But memorizing books is certainly not one of them*" (25; my emphasis). Sternberg adds that "active and engaged citizens must be creatively flexible, responding to rapid changes in the environment; able to think critically about what they are told in the media, whether by newscasters, politicians, advertisers, or scientists; able to execute their ideas and persuade others of their value; and, most of all, able to use their knowledge wisely in ways that avoid the horrors of bad leadership, as we have seen in scandals involving Enron, Arthur Anderson, Tyco, Clearstream, and innumerable other organizations" (25).

These skills, which are the foundation to making students "expert citizens," are what I want my students to acquire. These are the skills I want my two daughters to acquire, and I am guessing these are the skills you want your students and children to acquire. Unfortunately, these are not the skills emphasized in our schools today. As Sternberg points out, "Creativity, practical thinking, and wisdom are assessed minimally, or more likely, not at all" (2007/2008, 23). Why?

Because our students are so busy covering a vast and wide curriculum that little, if any, deeper thinking is occurring.

Jim Cox, former testing director in my school district, always reminded us to keep the following acronym in mind when planning instruction, "WYTI-WYG" (pronounced "witty-wig"): What You Test Is What You Get. Students immersed in massive test preparation classes receive massive amounts of shallow instruction. In the quest to raise scores and make teachers and administrators look good, our students are paying a price. Simply, a curriculum driven by multiple-choice assessments creates an oxymoron: many students are drowning in shallow "water." When instruction is driven by narrow assessment, instruction itself is narrowed. When students spend most of their time memorizing facts, their vital thinking skills, those skills foundational to turning them into "expert citizens," are buried. "When we teach only facts rather than how to go beyond the facts," Sternberg notes, "we are teaching students how to get out of date" (2007/2008, 21).

The Paige Paradox

A readicide curriculum limits all of our students' thinking, but under this siege of test preparation mentality, an interesting question should be considered: Which of our students are paying the steepest price?

The achievement gap in this country, most notably for low-income students and students of color (often, these are the same students), is no secret. Figure 1.1, for example, compiled by the Education Trust, illustrates the state-by-state achievement gap for African American students found in fourth- and eighth-grade reading scores.

By the fourth grade, African American students in thirteen states are already three years of learning behind grade level. By eighth grade, reading achievement for African American students remains two or more years behind grade level in thirty-six states. The numbers for Latino students aren't much better (see Figure 1.2).

It should also be noted that the achievement gap is not limited to reading skills. African American and Latino students also lag behind in their writing skills. Of course, we know that voluminous reading helps build strong writers, and a strong writing program helps build cognitive skills that help develop reading skills. (For a more in-depth study on this relationship, read Carol Booth Olson's *The Reading/Writing Connection* [2006].)

The Alliance for Excellent Education notes that "today fewer than a third of America's adolescents meet grade-level expectations for reading. Among

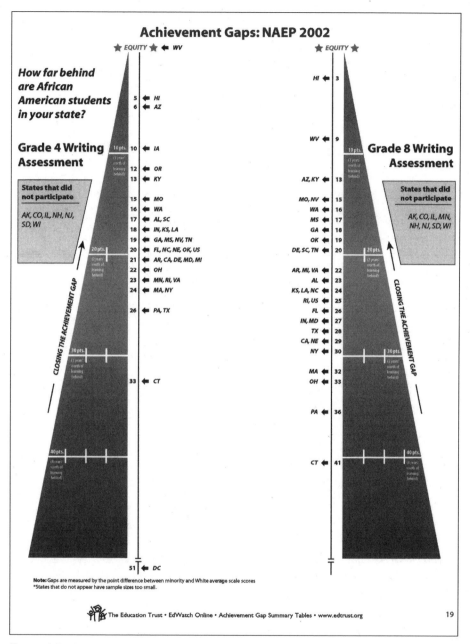

FIGURE 1.1
AFRICAN AMERICAN READING SCORES GRAPH (www.edtrust.org)

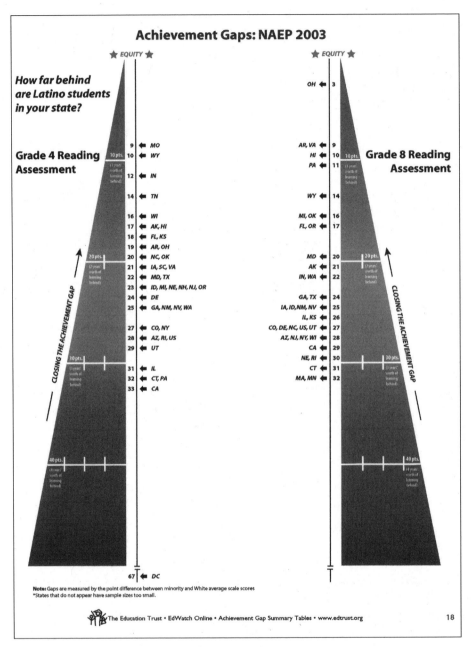

FIGURE 1.2
LATINO READING SCORES graph (www.edtrust.org)

low-income students, the number is closer to one in seven" (2007, 1). While there are numerous factors behind this achievement gap, let me suggest one major contributing factor: something I call the Paige Paradox, named after Rod Paige, secretary of education in the George W. Bush administration, and, therefore, may I suggest, the "father" of the readicide movement. The Paige Paradox goes something like this:

✖ A cornerstone to helping struggling readers is to measure their progress level every year via high-stakes multiple-choice tests. This approach will ensure that our struggling readers will rise to proficiency.
✖ State and national tests that value narrow thinking are put into place.
✖ Because the "worth" of teachers and administrators is largely perceived by how well students do on these shallow exams, educators narrow the curriculum in an all-out attempt to raise reading scores.
✖ Workbooks replace novels. Reading becomes another worksheet activity. Students are taught that the reason they should become readers is to pass a test.
✖ Reluctant readers drown in test preparation, ensuring any chance they may have had of developing a lifelong reading habit is lost. Worse than turning off to reading, students grow to hate reading.
✖ Students take the high-stakes tests. Students who already read well do fine. Students who do not read well fall into two categories:
  1. Those who come from test-preparation factories that impressively raise reading scores, thus sacrificing any chance of developing their students into lifelong readers or into deeper thinkers on the way; or
  2. Those who still read poorly and for the most part have long since given up.
✖ Schools receive their test scores. Schools with low-income students or a high percentage of students of color have the lowest scores.
✖ Schools that continue to struggle (often our worst-funded schools) are threatened with economic sanctions and other penalties. If they are given money, it is strictly earmarked for test preparation.
✖ Low-performing schools are threatened to increase the focus on the tests, thus forcing reluctant students into an even more shallow, mind-numbing curriculum. Because the approach did not work the first time, the approach the second time around is to take the ineffective approach and intensify it.
✖ Return to step one in the Paige Paradox. Continue this cycle until all reluctant readers are dead and all teachers are demoralized.

The paradox, of course, is found in the notion that the more students are "helped" in this cycle, the more likely readicide will occur (see Figure 1.3).

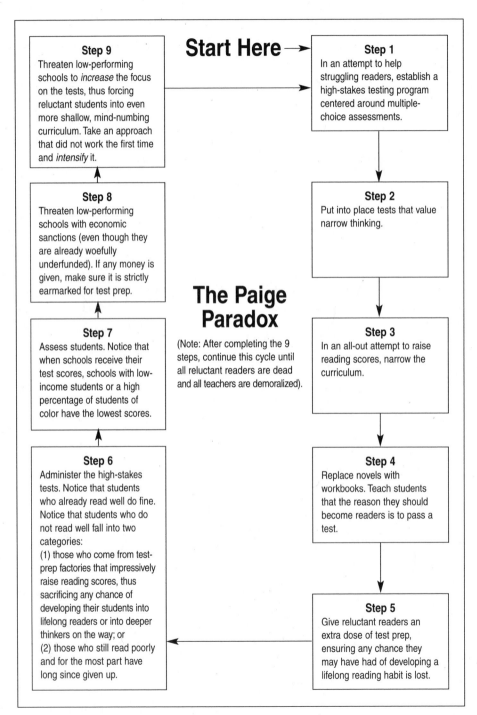

Step 9
Threaten low-performing schools to *increase* the focus on the tests, thus forcing reluctant students into even more shallow, mind-numbing curriculum. Take an approach that did not work the first time and *intensify* it.

Start Here →

Step 1
In an attempt to help struggling readers, establish a high-stakes testing program centered around multiple-choice assessments.

Step 8
Threaten low-performing schools with economic sanctions (even though they are already woefully underfunded). If any money is given, make sure it is strictly earmarked for test prep.

Step 2
Put into place tests that value narrow thinking.

The Paige Paradox

(Note: After completing the 9 steps, continue this cycle until all reluctant readers are dead and all teachers are demoralized).

Step 7
Assess students. Notice that when schools receive their test scores, schools with low-income students or a high percentage of students of color have the lowest scores.

Step 3
In an all-out attempt to raise reading scores, narrow the curriculum.

Step 6
Administer the high-stakes tests. Notice that students who already read well do fine. Notice that students who do not read well fall into two categories:
(1) those who come from test-prep factories that impressively raise reading scores, thus sacrificing any chance of developing their students into lifelong readers or into deeper thinkers on the way; or
(2) those who still read poorly and for the most part have long since given up.

Step 4
Replace novels with workbooks. Teach students that the reason they should become readers is to pass a test.

Step 5
Give reluctant readers an extra dose of test prep, ensuring any chance they may have had of developing a lifelong reading habit is lost.

FIGURE 1.3
THE PAIGE PARADOX

Texas Miracle or Texas Mirage?

This obsessive, national test-driven curriculum that leads our students to readi-cide is rooted in the "Texas Miracle"—the "remarkable" progress Texas schools made when educational carrots and sticks were attached to high-stakes, multiple-choice reading exams. (Rod Paige was superintendent of schools in Houston at the time and, as a result of the reading progress shown, parlayed these results into becoming President George W. Bush's choice for secretary of education.) As it turns out, the miraculous progress of students in Texas was not so miraculous. Many studies have revealed that the Texas Miracle—the model for teaching read-ing across our nation—is a sham. Teaching based on this reading model is prob-lematic on three fronts:

Problem 1: The results of the Texas Miracle are statistically flawed. In Texas high schools, the key test is given in the tenth grade. How did schools significantly raise tenth-grade scores? School officials did not count many students who gave up and dropped out. The Houston School District, for example, reported their dropout rate at 1.5 percent. Independent audits, however, actually estimated the dropout rate to be between 25 and 50 percent. Scads of struggling students disappeared and were not counted. Scores were raised, but it appears these drastic increases in test scores were achieved by keeping struggling readers from taking the tests (*60 Minutes II* 2004). In addition, of the at-risk students who remained, many were retained, some repeatedly, in the ninth grade as a means of preventing them from taking the tenth-grade test. After these students were kept in the ninth grade for two or more years, they were moved to the eleventh or twelfth grade, thus leapfrogging the crucial tenth-grade tests altogether (Gold 2008).

Problem 2: The pressures of the test fostered wide-scale cheating. When the stakes are high, incentive for cheating increases. In Texas, principals who raised reading scores were offered $5,000 bonuses. District administrators were offered up to $20,000. Because of these incentives, is it any surprise that the numbers were fudged? One example: at the height of the Texas Miracle, special education students were not counted in the test scores. Between 1994 and 1998, when the pressures on teachers and administrators was at a peak, the number of students who were designated as special education doubled, thus taking these students out of the equation. Walt Haney, a researcher in the Center for the Study of Testing, Evaluation, and Educational Policy at Boston University, notes that the exclusion of special education students accounts for a "substantial portion" of the apparent increases in pass rates of students in the 1990s (Haney 2000, 2).

Hiding kids under the special education umbrella appears to have been the primary reason that scores spiked.

An investigation by the *Dallas Morning News* examined elementary schools whose scores "swung wildly from year to year." The newspaper became suspicious when some schools made "jarring test-score leaps," vaulting from "mediocre to stellar in a single year." Worse, the paper found, when these elementary students moved on to middle school, their scores crashed. In the year that these students attended middle school, their scores went from the top 10 percent of all Texas schools to the bottom 10 percent in reading. "If the test scores are to be believed," the newspaper reported, "students at those schools lose much of their academic abilities as soon as they leave elementary school" (Benton and Hacker 2005). Interesting. Either the scores are real or they are not. If the scores are real, why would educators continue to teach in a way that results in students forgetting everything by the next year? If the scores are not real, which obviously seems to be the case, why would educators continue to teach this way at all? Of course, a reasonable person might ask, Do smart kids suddenly become unskilled in a year's time? Or is there is some funny manipulation of numbers occurring? Either way, the question remains, Why do we continue to subject students to this treatment?

Problem 3: The Texas treatment actually harmed students in the long run. In an exposé in the *Houston Chronicle*, reporter Melanie Markley (2004) cites the Aldine Independent School District, where all five high schools in the district were rated as "exemplary" or "recognized" by the state. Yet, while state test scores were rising at impressive rates, "Aldine's high schools reported a six-year drop on SAT scores, despite fewer students taking the test" (Markley 2004, A1). At the same time as their state scores were rising to impressive heights, "only about one-third of Aldine's graduates entering public colleges scored high enough on college readiness tests to avoid remedial classes" (Markley 2004, A1). Put another way, two out of three college-bound students, all from schools designated as "exemplary" or "recognized," did not have the skills necessary to take freshman-level college courses.

Haney, the Boston University researcher, notes that this phenomenon was not restricted to specific school districts. Statewide, while students were showing a 20 percent increase on state reading tests, there was a sharp decrease in their college readiness. Haney adds, that unlike SAT takers nationally, students in Texas have not improved on the SAT since the early 1990s (2000).

What's going on here? How could reading scores be rising at the same time that college readiness is dropping? Remember Jim Cox's WYTIWYG: What You Test Is What You Get. When teachers and students spend their energies preparing for shallow high-stakes assessments, deeper learning—the kind of thinking valued in colleges and the workforce—suffers. In this massive attempt to prepare all kids for college and the workforce, a readicide curriculum actually sets them back. In the almighty pursuit to get students to fill in "bubbles" on test sheets correctly, our students lose out on learning those skills that would make them "expert citizens": creativity, common sense, wisdom, ethics, dedication, honesty, teamwork, hard work, how to win and how to lose, fair play, and lifelong learning" (Sternberg 2007/2008). Instead, we get "higher" test scores and lower thinkers.

Jim Trelease, nationally acclaimed author of *The Read-Aloud Handbook*, best sums up the Texas Miracle when he says, "Building a national education agenda on the Texas model was like building a skyscraper on quicksand" (2008).

A Vicious Cycle

The research cited earlier in this chapter illustrates how a readicide curriculum harms college-bound students, but let's now take a moment to examine its effects on another subgroup: low-income students (many of whom will not go to college). I refer to the study that indicates that less than one in three students meets grade-level expectations in reading. That's appalling; however, for low-income students, the number rises to less than one in seven. Less than 14 percent of low-income students are reading at grade level. Clearly, the reading odds are stacked heavily against our students with the most severe needs.

In *Many Children Left Behind*, Theodore Sizer wrote, "The measure of the worth of a society is how it treats its weakest and most vulnerable citizens" (Meier et al. 2004, xvii). We must ask whether our approach to helping our weakest and most vulnerable students is working. Let's look at eighth-grade reading scores beginning in 2002, the first year of the No Child Left Behind Act, or NCLB:

Eighth-Grade Reading Scores

2002	264
2003	263
2005	262
2007	263

More telling are the scores for low-income eighth graders, which have remained unchanged:

Eighth-Grade Reading Scores for Low-Income Students	
2002	249
2003	247
2005	247
2007	247

The gap between the poor and the nonpoor has also remained unchanged:

Eighth-Grade Gap Between Poor and Nonpoor	
2002	23 points
2003	24 points
2005	23 points
2007	24 points

Why is the gap not closing? Maybe we should closely examine how we treat our struggling readers. It has been my experience that these students

✖ are often greeted by what Regie Routman, noted author and educator, refers to as the poverty of low expectations.
✖ are more likely to be placed in drill-and-kill reading remediation programs.
✖ are more likely to be placed in curriculums that heavily emphasize multiple-choice exams.
✖ have less access to interesting academic reading materials.
✖ have less access to high-interest recreational reading materials.
✖ often are not given time to read extensively.
✖ often are taught by the least-experienced teachers.

Is it any surprise, then, that struggling readers have a hard time overcoming their reading deficits? These approaches not only ensure that they will not catch up, but they also ensure that the achievement gap will widen as students move toward and through high school. This is exactly the phenomenon found by researchers from the Education Trust (2005) in *Gaining Traction, Gaining Ground*, a study that looked at factors that differentiate between "high impact" schools and "average impact" schools. The researchers "looked at high schools that are similar—in terms of demographics, and in terms of seeing a high percentage of students who struggled academically before entering high school. Generally, *such students tend to leave high school even further behind their peers*"

(30; my emphasis). We give struggling students a treatment that does not work, and worse, a treatment that turns them off to reading. When they perform poorly on mandated exams, we respond by giving them an intensified dose of the ineffective treatment. And before we know it, we find ourselves once again smack in the middle of the Paige Paradox. The result: students enter high school behind in reading and leave even farther behind in reading. Worse, many leave our schools hating reading, arguably the single most important skill we want our students to value as they head into adulthood.

The irony, of course, is seen when one remembers the stated goal of NCLB: that every student in the United States be proficient in reading by 2014. It appears the opposite may be occurring. One 2007 study (TIMSS & PIRLS International Study Center) also found that fourth graders in the United States have lost ground in reading ability compared with students around the world. The global reading test was administered in 2001 (one year before NCLB) and again in 2006. American students showed no gains in reading, despite the emphasis on NCLB. While American students were mired in a readicide approach, they dropped farther behind other countries, falling from the fourth highest scores in the world in 2001 to tenth place in 2006 (see http://timss.bc.edu/ for the complete analysis). In an era in which our students will be competing for jobs in a global marketplace, our current approach to teaching reading promises long-lasting, deleterious effects on both our children and our nation.

Diane Ravitch, professor of education at New York University and noted education researcher, says it best:

> *Congress should drop the absurd goal of achieving universal proficiency by 2014. Given that no nation, no state, and no school district has ever reached 100 percent math and reading proficiency for all grades, it is certain that the goal cannot be met. Perpetuating this unrealistic ideal, however, guarantees that increasing numbers of schools will "fail" as the magic year 2014 gets closer.* (2007)

Researchers at the National Center for Fair and Open Testing (2007) agree. They predict that under the current accountability system, 70 to 100 percent of all schools will, sooner or later, "fail."

Let's see whether we have this straight: we immerse students in a curriculum that drives the love of reading out of them, prevents them from developing into deeper thinkers, ensures the achievement gap will remain, reduces their college readiness, and guarantees that the result will be that our schools will fail.

We have lost our way. It is time to stop the madness.

What You Can Do to Prevent Readicide

When I codirected the South Basin Writing Project site, we began each morning by discussing the burning issues that arose from our ongoing research. Often these burning issues led to "hard talk" that was sure to generate passions and disagreement. If we have any chance of addressing readicide, we must involve the key players (teachers, students, administrators, literacy coaches, superintendents, board members, legislators, newspaper reporters) in hard talk. We have to take an honest, perhaps painful, look at what is happening to young readers in our schools. We have to be ready to step on toes and be prepared to have our own toes stepped on.

To help facilitate the hard talk that may lead to a change in our practices, I suggest beginning with the following questions (see also the Hard Talk Checklist on page 135):

✖ What do we mean when we say our school "values" reading?

✖ Is our quest for higher test scores harming our students' long-term reading prospects?

✖ Why is it that the higher the grade level, the higher the chances that students are turned off to reading?

✖ Are our students being trained to think deeply? Is width drowning depth? Which world is more important for us, as teachers, to heed—the political world or the authentic world?

✖ Are we out of balance? (authentic versus political)

✖ Is our treatment of struggling readers helping to lift them out of the remedial reading track? Or are the same students mired in remedial classes year after year? Is our treatment working?

✖ Are remedial readers even farther behind when they leave high school than they were when they entered high school?

✖ Are we losing more and more readers every year? Is the percentage of students who love reading dwindling? What might be occurring inside our school that may be contributing to this phenomenon?

✖ Are our students doing enough academic reading? If not, why not? What can we do to change the downward trend?

✖ Are our students doing enough recreational reading? If not, why not? What can we do to change the downward trend?

✖ Are we giving our students the kinds of reading experiences that lead them to be "expert citizens"? (Sternberg 2007/2008, 21)

✖ Are we stuck in the vicious cycle of the Paige Paradox?

✖ Do we understand that intensive focus on state tests has not translated into deeper reading on other assessments, such as the SAT or National Assessment of Educational Progress? Do we understand that there is evidence that this focus actually decreases college readiness?

✖ Do we understand that since NCLB began, reading scores have remained flat and that the achievement gap has remained wide?

✖ Do we understand that the goal of this testing madness—every student will be proficient by 2014—is unattainable and is used as a hammer to push more students into a readicide curriculum?

✖ Do we agree with Diane Ravitch, who notes, "Unless we set realistic goals for our schools and adopt realistic means of achieving them, we run the risk of seriously damaging education and leaving almost all children behind"? (2007)

Hard talk is a starting point in addressing readicide. But it is just a start. Subsequent chapters in this book will address, in depth, other steps you can take to eliminate readicide, but before closing this chapter, let me conclude by sharing some of Judith A. Langer's findings from an in-depth study conducted at twenty-five schools in California, New York, Florida, and Texas. Langer identifies two types of schools—those that were found to be "'beating the odds,' that is, scoring higher on high-stakes tests than students in demographically comparable schools," and those schools she deemed as "typical" (2002, 3). Langer found that schools exhibit three distinct instructional approaches, patterns she has named (1) separated, (2) simulated, and (3) integrated. Separated instruction is the direct instruction of isolated skills, often used to "cover" curriculum. Simulated instruction "involves the application of these concepts and rules within a targeted unit of reading, writing, or oral language" (Langer 2002, 13). This might include, for example, exercises that are often found in packaged teaching materials. Integrated instruction "takes place when students are expected to use their skills and knowledge within the embedded context of a large and purposeful activity," such as writing a research paper or editing the school newspaper (Langer 2002, 14). Though Langer found that these instructional approaches are widespread, the "amounts and orchestrations" of these instructional approaches differed widely between effective schools and typical schools. In short, effective schools did not rely heavily on any given approach, often blending all three types of instruction. Typical schools, however, were found to rely on one dominant approach only. Langer's key point? Schools that rely solely on any one approach are unlikely to rise to the level of an effective school. This research has a lot to say to schools that immerse fragile readers heavily into test preparation or scripted programs.

Langer's research uncovered some other interesting differences between effective and typical schools:

"Beating the Odds" Schools Versus "Typical" Schools

"Beating the Odds" Schools	*"Typical" Schools*
"Test preparation does not mean mere practice of test related items. Rather the focus is on the underlying knowledge and skills needed to do well in coursework and in life." (17)	"Test prep means test practice. It is allocated its own space in class time, often before testing begins, apart from the rest of the year's work and goals" (17)
Lessons have relevance to students' lives, often connecting the learning to other classrooms, as well as with the outside world.	There is often little weaving of lessons into other units or other subjects. Units of instruction are treated as "separate wholes" (26).
Students are taught strategies for thinking as well as doing.	"The focus is on content or skill, without overtly teaching the overarching strategies for planning, organizing, completing, or reflecting on the content or activity" (28).
"The tenor of the instructional environment is such that, even after students reach instructional goals, English language arts teachers move students beyond them toward deeper understanding of and ability to generate ideas and knowledge" (32–33).	"Once students exhibit use of the immediate understandings or skills in focus, teachers move on to another lesson" (33).
"English learning and high literacy (the content as well as the skills) are treated as a social activity with depth and complexity." (36) Students participate in numerous meaningful discussions about their reading and writing.	"Students tend to work alone or interact with the teacher, and when collaboration or group work occurs, the activity focuses on answering questions rather than in engaging in substantive discussion from multiple perspectives" (36).

Langer's study, and the many others cited in this chapter, leads to an inescapable conclusion: if students are taught to read and write well, they will do fine on mandated reading tests. But if they are only taught to be test-takers, they will never learn to read and write well. A terrible price is paid when schools value the development of test-takers more than they value the development of readers.

Endangered Minds

Recently, my twelfth-grade students were reading *All Quiet on the Western Front*, and as part of the unit, I had given them two editorials—one arguing that the United States should immediately withdraw from Iraq, the other arguing that the "surge" strategy was working and that America should stay and fight. As a first step to making meaning from the articles, I had provided the students with highlighters and directions to highlight anything that confused them on their first-draft reading. After they identified their confusion, students collaborated in groups to work through their rough spots. Circulating through the room, I noticed Marissa and Justine struggling with a passage they both had highlighted as a trouble spot.

> "Mr. Gallagher, can you help us?" Marissa asked as I approached.
>
> "What's troubling you?" I replied.
>
> "Neither one of us gets this part," Justine explained, pointing to the passage that both girls had highlighted. "We don't get what it means when it mentions 'the lifeblood of al Qaeda.'"
>
> "What do you think it might mean?" I replied. "Look at the context of the sentence."
>
> "How should we know?" Marissa said. "We don't even know who this Al guy is."
>
> "Yes," Justine added. "Who is this Al guy?

I wanted to smile but, fortunately, caught myself in time when I realized they were not pulling my leg. Both of these students—both high school seniors, both old enough to vote in the upcoming presidential election—thought "Al" Qaeda was a person. At that time, the United States had been at war for five and a half years, and here were two students, two young adults leaving the educational system, who had never heard of al Qaeda. Both, by the way, had passed the multiple-choice reading section of the state's high school exit exam.

The "Al" Qaeda anecdote is not an isolated incident. At the time I was writing this book, for example, the 2008 presidential primaries were unfolding; yet, out of my thirty-eight freshman students, only one student could identify John McCain, John Edwards, Mitt Romney, Mike Huckabee, or Rudy Giuliani. Perhaps more unbelievable was that only one of my ninth graders could name the sitting vice president of the United States. Worse, only six of my 100 seniors— again, people old enough to vote—could identify Dick Cheney. This is not a problem found only in urban California schools. I shared this story with a group of teachers in Northern Virginia, just a few minutes from Washington, D.C., and one government teacher said that only five of his seniors could identify the vice president. Only five from a group of high school seniors living in the shadow of the nation's capital! Despite this, my guess is that most of his students also passed their state reading exams.

Something is seriously wrong with this picture.

Students Need Authentic Reading

I literally wrote this paragraph 35,000 feet above Arizona. It was a beautiful day, and the pilot had just announced that passengers sitting on the right-hand side of the plane would have a "spectacular" view of the Grand Canyon. Unfortunately, I was sitting on the left-hand side of the plane, straining to see any hint of the natural wonder outside my window. My window was too narrow, so I missed the show.

I couldn't help but wonder whether my flight would be an apt metaphor for what is happening to our students. They were receiving a heavy dose of reading but through a narrow window. They could see the upcoming tests through the window, of course, but in narrowing their reading experiences to focus on test preparation, we were ensuring they would miss the larger show. By gearing students year in and year out to practice for state-mandated reading exams, we had begun producing high school seniors (students who now had numerous years of testing focus) who had passed their reading tests but were leaving our schools without the cultural literacy needed to be productive citizens in a democratic society. They could "bubble" in the correct answers, but to mix the metaphor, they were unaware what was happening on the other side of the airplane. This raises an alarming question: Can we afford to graduate students who are so intensely geared toward reading exams that they leave our schools never having had the opportunity to look out the other reading windows?

This chapter will argue that our students are in desperate need of large doses of authentic reading—the kinds of reading we, as adults, do in newspapers, magazines, blogs, and websites. These doses need to come from a mix of reading experiences, from longer, challenging novels and works of nonfiction to "lighter" recreational reading. Our students should be reading through many windows, not just a single, narrow window that gives them a view of the next exam.

The first step in broadening our students' reading windows comes when we recognize the three factors that serve as major contributors to readicide:

1. There is a dearth of interesting reading materials in our schools.
2. Many schools have removed novels and other longer challenging works to provide teachers and students with more test preparation time.
3. Students are not doing enough reading in school.

This chapter will examine each of these factors and conclude with specific suggestions on how to turn the tide of readicide. Let's begin with the first and most important factor.

Readicide Factor: There Is a Dearth of Interesting Reading Materials in Our Schools

I was channel surfing in a hotel one evening when I came across a documentary about America's most underrated athlete, Olympic champion swimmer Michael Phelps. Though I don't know much about competitive swimming, I found the show fascinating. Swimmers at that level of competition work out for hours every day, week after week, month after month, year after year, to get to a single race where the difference between gold and silver is often one one-hundredth of a second. Amazing. As I was watching the gold medal race, the eight swimmers were desperately churning, neck and neck, to be the first to touch the wall. Now remember, I do not know much about swimming, but as they were driving to the finish line, I was struck by an idea: each swimmer, long before that Olympic race, had daily access to a pool. I am overstating the obvious, I know, but it helps to raise a key point when it comes to readicide. An Olympic swimmer swims hundreds of thousands of laps before he is judged in the medal race. It would be ludicrous for Phelps to blow off his training only to decide at the last minute to show up poolside at the Olympics to try to win a gold medal. He knows that a tremendous amount of practice is a nonnegotiable prerequisite to performing well.

The Michael Phelps anecdote reminds me of what is happening to our students. We put them in the "race" (in this case, high-stakes reading tests) and ask them to perform well. However, there is a big problem: these students have not been in the "pool" very much. They are being asked to perform at high levels even though many of them haven't been doing much authentic reading. Many haven't even put their toes in the water. If we want kids to become better readers, they have to read a lot more than they are currently reading. And if we want our students to do a lot more reading than they are currently doing, they need to be immersed in a pool of high-interest reading material.

Unfortunately, putting good books in front of our students has not been the focus in many of our nation's schools. I teach at a high school in Anaheim, and there is not a single bookstore in the community where I teach. (Anaheim must be the largest city in the country without either a Barnes and Noble or a Borders bookstore.) To make matters worse, my students come from print-poor environments. Under these circumstances, shouldn't schools be the place where students interact with interesting books? Shouldn't the faculty have an ongoing, laser-like commitment to put good books in our students' hands? Shouldn't this be a front-burner issue at all times?

Sadly, this is not happening. When was the last time your faculty had a substantive discussion about whether students have sufficient access to interesting reading materials? You would think that would be the first item of concern at the beginning of a new school year, but that is not the case. When I ask teachers how often they discuss acquiring interesting reading material in faculty meetings, the answer can be summed up with one word: infrequently. At my school, for example, the topics we discussed at the first faculty meeting two days before the start of school were as follows:

✖ A review of employee health benefits
✖ A review of how to call in for a substitute teacher
✖ A review of student referral forms
✖ A review of the attendance policy
✖ A review of the school's discipline plan
✖ A review of the district's grading policies
✖ A review of student progress report forms

✖ A review of the school's voicemail system
✖ A review of the district's email policy
✖ A review of the school's moment-of-silence policy
✖ A review of how to fill out employee health cards
✖ A review of the district's new paycheck system
✖ A review of the district's drug and alcohol policy
✖ A review of the district's sexual harassment policy
✖ A review of our Academic Performance Index (API) and Academic Yearly Progress (AYP) scores from last year (but no time spent exploring what we might do about the scores)
✖ A reminder to have our faculty photos taken
✖ A reminder to take certain security measures
✖ A reminder for teachers to check their mailboxes at least twice a day
✖ An explanation of an on-site car wash service for teachers
✖ An explanation of the new teacher evaluation forms
✖ A discussion regarding Back-to-School Night
✖ A discussion regarding budget concerns
✖ A discussion of items that need to be placed on teachers' calendars
✖ Directions on how to submit a morning announcement to be read on the school's public address system
✖ An overview of a new automated home contact system
✖ A staff survey
✖ Three assistant principals shared their concerns
✖ The counseling department shared their concerns

Three hours and twenty-eight agenda items later, reading had not been mentioned. No discussion about what might be leading to low reading test scores. Not one hint on what we might do to move students into deeper reading. No concern about the profound lack of interesting reading materials in students' homes, in our community, and on our campus. Two days before school began, and it was as though no reading problems existed on our campus. On the bright side, I left the meeting knowing when and where I could get my car washed every Friday.

It always amazes (and depresses) me that grown, educated adults can sit in a room and argue endlessly over whether a student's pants are too baggy or whether a student should be marked tardy if he or she is not yet seated when the bell rings. I am not making this up. One year the teachers in my school spent an entire year arguing about what color to paint our school. And every time we had one of those discussions, I thought about the classrooms a few feet away missing the one thing our students desperately need: interesting books.

Let me be clear: if we are to have any chance of developing a reading habit in our students, they must be immersed in a K–12 "book flood"—a term coined by researcher Warwick Elley (1991). Students must have ready access to a wide range of interesting reading materials. This goal should be the priority of every faculty. I discussed this in greater length in my first two books, *Reading Reasons* (2003) and *Deeper Reading* (2004), but the idea is worth restating when one considers what happens when students cannot get their hands on great books. We must start all discussions about the state of reading on our campuses with a simple, direct question: do our students have ample access to high-interest reading materials?

The Danger of Word Poverty

The importance of access to language emerges early in our students' lives. In *Proust and the Squid: The Story and Science of the Reading Brain*, Maryanne Wolf (2007) notes that "by kindergarten, a gap of 32 million words already separates some children in linguistically impoverished homes from their more stimulated peers. In other words, in some environments the average young middle-class child hears 32 million more spoken words than the young underprivileged child by age five" (20). A gap that forms before students even start school snowballs once school begins. As Wolf notes,

> *It is not simply a matter of the number of words unheard and unlearned. When words are not heard, concepts are not learned. When syntactic forms are never encountered, there is less knowledge about the relationship of events in a story. When story forms are never known, there is less ability to infer and predict. When cultural traditions and the feelings of others are never experienced, there is less understanding of what other people feel.* (2007, 102)

By the third grade, students who suffer from "word poverty" are often at a million-word reading deficit; by the sixth grade, they are already three grade levels behind their average-performing peers.

People who are undernourished need good food. Readers who are undernourished need good books. Lots of them. Instead, what do many undernourished readers get? They are often placed in remedial classes where the pace is slowed and where the reading focus moves away from books to a steady diet of small chunks of reading. In an effort to "help" prepare them for reading tests, we

FIGURE 2.1
BRIDGE TO PRISON

starve readers. Rather than lift up struggling readers, this approach contributes to widening the achievement gap.

Let's take a moment to explore how narrowing the curriculum to spend more time on reading practice actually harms the building of young readers. For example, a reader needs to understand approximately 90 percent of the words found in a passage to comprehend the reading. Less commonly known is that the reader's knowledge of the world factors into making sense of print. What the reader brings to the page is often more important than the ability to read the words on the page. To illustrate this, read Figure 2.1.

I have shown this cartoon to adults in numerous workshops, and every adult can read the cartoon. Every person can read "Bridge to Prison." Every person has been able to read the word "Stevens" on the side of the car. In reading the cartoon, no one is tripped up by phonemic awareness or fluency problems. In short, reading the cartoon is not a problem. Comprehending the cartoon, however, is another matter. Though I have found almost everyone capable of reading the cartoon, few adult readers understand it, because to comprehend this cartoon you first have to know a number of things. To understand the Bridge to Prison cartoon, for example, you'd have to be aware of the events that were going on in the country when it was drawn:

✖ Alaskan Senator Ted Stevens, securing more than $200 million in public funding, championed a proposed bridge to be built between Gravina Island and the town of Ketchican.

✖ In September 2007, it was cancelled.

✖ In July 2008, Stevens, the longest-serving Republican senator and a figure in Alaska politics since before statehood, was indicted on seven counts of failing to disclose thousands of dollars in services he received from a company that helped renovate his home.

✖ The proposed bridge would have cost taxpayers $329 million.

✖ The project, dubbed the "Bridge to Nowhere," quickly became a national symbol of federal pork barrel spending.

Knowing these points before reading the cartoon enables the reader to comprehend it. Students who have not read voluminously may never have heard of the Bridge to Nowhere. They probably would not know what "pork barrel spending" means. More than likely, they never would have heard of Senator Stevens. Yes, they might be able to "read" the cartoon, but without the proper knowledge foundation, they will not understand it.

The Bridge to Prison cartoon reminds us that reading consists of two factors: (1) being able to decode words on the page and (2) being able to connect the words you are reading with the prior knowledge you bring to the page. When schools narrow reading to "help" students prepare for tests, or cut social studies, science, or electives to raise reading scores, they are removing invaluable opportunities for students to widen and deepen knowledge that is foundational to developing readers. Without a broad knowledge base, our students stand no chance of being excellent readers.

Unfortunately, as E. D. Hirsch (2006) points out in *The Knowledge Deficit: Closing the Shocking Education Gap for American Children*, schools are reluctant to commit to the goal of building prior knowledge:

> *Most current reading programs talk about activating the reader's background knowledge so she can comprehend a text. But in practice, they are only paying lip service to the well-known scientific finding that background knowledge is essential to reading comprehension. Little attempt is made to enlarge the child's background knowledge.* (Hirsch 2006, 72)

Hirsch is right, but he is too gentle. When schools remove books in favor of practice tests, when schools eliminate subjects such as science and history, when schools drown students in test preparation, they are ensuring students will not become excellent readers. Instead of enlarging the background knowledge, quite the opposite occurs. This approach shrinks our students' understanding of the world. Students may pass the tests, but they're being robbed of perhaps the only opportunity they may ever have of building that wide knowledge base that is foundational if they are to develop into critical readers of the world. In the fevered quest to raise test scores, schools are irreparably harming young readers, especially readers who have already begun school suffering from word poverty.

The opposite approach, of course, is that by providing a wide and deep reading experience, we actually help students raise their test scores (without inflicting readicide). In a famous study of fifth graders, Anderson, Wilson, and Fielding (1998) found a strong correlation between time spent reading and performance on standardized reading tests.

Percentage Rank	Minutes of Reading per Day	Estimated Number of Words Read per Year
98	90.7	4,733,000
90	40.4	2,357,000
70	21.7	1,168,000
50	12.9	601,000
20	3.1	134,000
10	1.6	51,000

More recently, in *To Read or Not to Read*, a study conducted by the National Endowment for the Arts (2007), researchers reached the same conclusion. Students who read the most for fun scored the highest on standardized reading tests:

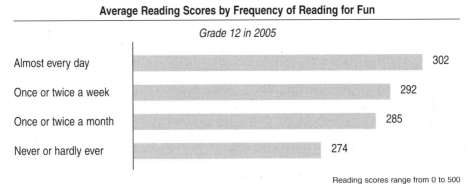

Average Reading Scores by Frequency of Reading for Fun

Grade 12 in 2005

Almost every day	302
Once or twice a week	292
Once or twice a month	285
Never or hardly ever	274

Reading scores range from 0 to 500

Source: U.S. Department of Education, National Center for Education Statistics (2005).

Students who read the most for fun also had the highest writing scores:

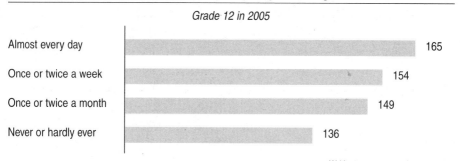

Average Writing Scores by Frequency of Reading for Fun

Grade 12 in 2005

Almost every day	165
Once or twice a week	154
Once or twice a month	149
Never or hardly ever	136

Writing scores range from 0 to 300

Source: U.S. Department of Education, National Center for Education Statistics (2005).

Not surprisingly, these studies demonstrate that students who have the broadest reading experiences score the highest on standardized tests. Conversely, those students with the narrowest reading experiences scored the lowest. Clearly, if we want students to perform well on standardized reading tests, our top priority should not be in narrowing students into a test-prep curriculum; our focus should be on providing our students with the widest reading experiences possible.

The Importance of Knowledge Capital

Reading tests don't just measure a student's understanding of the words on the page; they also largely measure what a student brings to the page. This was illustrated recently when my students sat down to take the state's high school exit exam, a prerequisite for graduation. As they filed in to take the test, there was a sense of nervousness in the air. I was also a bit on edge, especially when I saw Matt walk in the door.

Matt is one of those kids who rarely attends school. He lives with his mom, who is a drug addict, and he has never met his father. Matt is not a reader, and he is unskilled in language arts. He is unfocused in class and often carries an undercurrent of anger with him. As I said, he rarely attends school, so I was surprised to see him show up on test day. Frankly, I was also concerned that he would drag down my class average. (Isn't that, in itself, a sad commentary on how testing twists teachers' brains? Here is a kid who needs school more than anyone else in the class, and I was actually sorry to see him show up to class on that particular day.) Because Matt had not been in class much, I was particularly worried about his reading endurance, so as he began taking the exam I kept him in my line of vision. He started strong, but it wasn't long before Matt began what I call "The Reader's Melt." By the second passage and set of questions, he had begun sliding down in his chair. When he turned the pages to the third passage in his booklet, he gave up, let out a derisive snort, and skipped the passage entirely (not a strategy, by the way, that I had been emphasizing in class).

After the answer sheets were turned in I pulled Matt aside and told him I had noticed that he had skipped an entire section of the test. The conversation went something like this:

Mr. Gallagher: Matt, I noticed you skipped a section of the test. Right?
Matt: Yep.
Mr. G: Why did you do that?
Matt: Did you see what that section of the test was called?
Mr. G: No. What was it called?
Matt: The Farrier . . . I didn't know what that was, so I skipped it.

After Matt left, I retrieved a test booklet and found the passage in question. To be honest, looking at the title, I did not know what a farrier was either, so I read the passage. It didn't take too long to figure it out; the first sentence read: "A farrier, a person who makes a living by putting shoes on horses, can make a good living." The farrier sentence piqued my interest, so later that day I began my three senior classes by asking how many students knew the definition of a farrier. Out of ninety-nine urban, Southern Californian twelfth graders, not a single student knew the word. Not one. Not knowing the word myself, I was not surprised.

However, here is where the story gets interesting: two days later, I was demonstrating a lesson in a high school classroom in Wyoming. Before beginning the lesson, I asked the students how many of them could tell me what a farrier was. Hands shot up. Almost every student in the classroom knew the word. Now I only spent a short time with these students, and I could be wrong, but I sensed they were very much like my own students—not superstar readers, not illiterate, more aliterate than anything else. They know how to read, but outside of school, they rarely choose to do so.

When I arrived back at school the next day, I told my classes how the students in Wyoming knew the word *farrier*. "I found that interesting," I told them. "Seeing how none of you knew the word, I have come to a simple conclusion: students in Wyoming are smarter than you." This, of course, started an interesting argument that led to the key point I wanted my students to consider. It isn't that the students in Wyoming are necessarily smarter than my students in California; it's just that their experiences growing up in Wyoming have varied greatly from the experiences of kids who grow up in a major city. They grew up with horses; my students didn't.

I am not defending Matt's choice to skip "The Farrier" passage. But I think the story points out the importance that prior knowledge plays when a reader approaches a page. If I teach "The Farrier" in Wyoming, I can hand it to the students and get started immediately, but if I teach this story in Anaheim, as the teacher, I need to frame the text before their reading commences. These kids in Wyoming and in Anaheim might have the same reading abilities, but that doesn't mean they are on equal footing when the reading starts. Kids without prior knowledge are at a disadvantage, regardless of reading ability.

The importance of what a reader brings to the page is also highlighted in a study discussed by Hirsch in *The Knowledge Deficit* (2006). This study consisted of two groups of students who were asked to read a passage about baseball. The first group was made up of strong readers who knew little about baseball. The second group was composed of struggling readers who were knowledgeable about baseball. After reading the passage, students in each group had their comprehension tested. Guess which group scored higher? The struggling readers. Having strong reading skills was not enough for the students who came to the page with a knowledge deficit about the topic. Though the second group of readers were not strong readers, the prior knowledge they brought to the page enabled them to outscore readers with far better abilities. Prior knowledge, or, in the case of the good readers, the lack of prior knowledge, was the x-factor (Hirsch 2006).

I do not know whether this year's state test will have a passage about baseball or farriers, but I do know one thing: those students who sit down to the exam with the broadest base of prior knowledge will have the highest chances of scoring well. If we are serious about building strong readers, we need to be serious about building strong knowledge foundations in our students. With this in mind, we should be mindful of the large wealth of knowledge capital that comes from the voluminous reading of books, newspapers, blogs, and magazines. These are the sources that build the critical foundations of serious readers, and knowing the value of these sources returns us to some crucial questions for educators at your school to consider. Do students at your school have access to a wide range of interesting reading materials? Is providing access to interesting text a priority among your administration and faculty? Are students on your campus immersed in a book flood? Are we giving them every opportunity, via reading, to build vital knowledge capital? Are these questions even addressed during your faculty meetings?

Readicide Factor: Many Schools Have Removed Novels and Other Longer Challenging Works to Provide Teachers and Students with More Test Preparation Time

I have begun to notice a troubling trend with many of my adolescent readers over the past few years. Most of these students can "read," but when it comes time to think deeply about what they have read, they have difficulty diving below the surface. They can regurgitate text on a literal level, but increasingly, they have trouble with heavier intellectual lifting (e.g., evaluating, analyzing, synthesizing). They can find information on a moment's notice on the Internet, but they have trouble getting past a surface-level understanding of the text they retrieve. In short, they know a lot, but they understand little. This phenomenon is not limited to my classroom in Anaheim; I hear this same concern from teachers across the country.

Jane Healy, author of *Endangered Minds: Why Children Can't Think—and What We Can Do About It* (1990), notes that as children grow, they have very distinct developmental needs. She states, "Neuroscience suggests strongly that if the child's developmental needs during these periods are not met, we may actually close down some of those developmental windows" (Healy 1990, 2–3). Like many parents and teachers, Healy is concerned about the effects of television and video games on our children's brains, especially when they are in these key cognitive developmental windows. It is no coincidence, Healy suggests, that alongside the advent of television and computer games, there has been a drastic increase in the number of children diagnosed with attention deficit disorder. And though "certain brains have constitutional difficulty in paying attention, our culture is not helping those brains develop strategies for attention and it may be pushing some kids off the deep end who wouldn't be there otherwise" (Healy 1990, 2). Outside of school, many of our students are not partaking in those critical activities that stretch and deepen their brains. Instead, they often gravitate to those behaviors that offer instant gratification. As a result, Healy notes, many children are literally starving the lobes of the prefrontal cortex of their brains, a starvation Healy characterizes as "frightening."

If our students' neurological windows are shutting down, then school may be the only place where they are given an opportunity to build up the key parts of their brains that need to be developed before acquiring the ability to think deeply. Unfortunately, the trend in our schools is in the opposite direction. Healy laments that in today's schools, students "are not allowed to sit and think. They are constantly rammed through a curriculum to see how fast we can move them along. As they are marched from activity to activity, even the schedule of the school day doesn't allow time for anyone to reflect. And coming up with solutions is quite different from the type of thinking required to be successful on some of the so-called achievement tests" (Healy 1990, 4). Schools, she adds, "are very out of sync with what's going to be needed in our thinking for the next century, and, in fact, is desperately needed right now" (4).

When schools remove novels from the students' curriculum and replace challenging books with shorter pieces and worksheets, they are denying students the foundational reading experiences for developing those regions of their brains that enable them to think deeply. As Wolf states, "To acquire [reading skills] children need instructional environments that support all the circuit parts that need bolting for the brain to read. Such a perspective departs from current teaching methods that focus largely on only one or two major components of reading" (2007, 19). When we deny students the opportunity to read long, complex works, we are starving a part of their brains, and we start producing kids like the students in my class who can read but who cannot get below the surface of what they read.

Administrators who remove novels from the curriculum do not understand the harm they are inflicting on adolescents. Novels are not part of the problem; the problem lies in how the novels are taught. Any teacher worth his salt can teach any language arts standard through teaching any novel. I can teach students to recognize themes whether they are reading *Romeo and Juliet* or *The Great Gatsby*. I can teach students to write an analytical essay whether they are reading *Hamlet* or *Animal Farm*. I can teach students to stand up and deliver an argument whether they are reading *1984* or *Of Mice and Men*.

Unfortunately, I have had administrators in my career who do not understand this. They think that when I teach novels my kids are "just reading stories." I actually had an administrator ask me one time to stop reading the novel so my kids could start practicing their "critical thinking skills." Administrators who remove novels from the curriculum do not understand that when we teach the standards through complex novels, the benefits to students are twofold: they not only learn the standards but also develop the deepest regions of their brains. They stretch their brains to read longer, more challenging works.

Starving the part of the brain that needs to be developed before deeper reading can occur also has consequences outside the classroom. Readicide has long-lasting ramifications beyond the school years. As Healy wonders, "Are we going to have an entire generation of people who cannot manage their own behavior, manage their world, plan ahead, reflect on abstract ideas, or relate appropriately to moral and social and ethical issues?" (1990, 4). These concerns arise when the brain is not given every opportunity to develop. The window shuts. If we want to keep these windows from shutting, if we want our students to be complex thinkers, they need to be challenged to read long, complex texts. Instead of removing novels from the curriculum, we should be giving them *more* novels to read. Far from being part of the problem, novels should be seen as part of the solution.

Many people might construe my argument about the importance of novels as a call for removing large anthology series from the curriculum. In the interest of full disclosure, I am a consultant for a national anthology program. I use anthologies in my classroom and find them to be valuable. I object to districts that remove novels so that the only reading done by students is short pieces out of an anthology. I don't use the anthology in my classroom as the entire curriculum. I use the rich short stories and poems in the anthology to augment the novels my students are reading. My students read both long and short pieces, because I want them to exercise all regions of their reading brains.

Readicide Factor: Students Are Not Doing Enough Reading in School

According to *To Read or Not to Read* (National Endowment for the Arts 2007), Americans are reading less. Consider the following:

✖ Less than one-third of thirteen-year-olds are daily readers, a 14 percent decline from twenty years earlier.

✖ Among seventeen-year-olds, the percentage of nonreaders has more than doubled over a twenty-year period, from 9 percent in 1984 to 19 percent in 2004.

✖ The percentage of thirteen-year-olds who read for fun on a daily basis declined from 35 percent to 30 percent, and for seventeen-year-olds the decline was from 33 percent to 22 percent.

✖ On average, Americans ages fifteen to twenty-four spend almost two hours a day watching television, and only seven minutes of their leisure time on reading.

✖ Nearly half of all Americans ages fifteen to twenty-four do not read books for pleasure.

For anyone in the classroom, these findings are not a surprise. The more important question, of course, is what we can do in our classrooms to turn the tide.

One of the casualties of this testing era seems to be the death of sustained
silent reading (SSR). As I travel across the country, I see that SSR has been
removed from schools to give students more time to prepare for exams. SSR has
clearly fallen out of favor, which is unfortunate because eliminating SSR is
wrongheaded for three reasons:

SSR is actually a valuable investment in test preparation. In *The Power of
Reading: Insights from the Research*, Stephen Krashen (1993b) notes:

✖ In 38 of 41 studies, students given free voluntary reading (FVR) time did as
   well as or better in reading comprehension tests than students given traditional skill-based reading instruction (2).
✖ The longer FVR is practiced, the more consistent the results (3).
✖ Reading as a leisure activity is the best predictor of comprehension, vocabulary, and reading speed (5). Kids who do the most recreational reading
   become the best readers.
✖ Reading is too complex to learn one rule at a time (14).

Interestingly, after Krashen's book was published, the National Reading Panel
stated that no definitive study proved that FVR has a positive effect on reading
comprehension. This finding interested Yi-Chen Wu and S. Jay Samuels (2004),
researchers at the University of Minnesota, who conducted a study of their own.
Their findings flew in the face of the National Reading Panel:

✖ "More time spent reading had a significant effect on achievement compared to
   a control condition where less time was allotted for recreational reading" (2).
✖ "Poor readers showed significantly greater gain in word recognition and
   vocabulary than good readers" (2).
✖ "Poor readers tended to have greater gains in vocabulary with 15 minutes of
   reading" and "they had better gains on reading comprehension with 40 minutes of reading" (2).

Wu and Samuels (2004) also cite a number of studies that found a high correlation between the amount of independent reading time and students' reading
achievement scores. Krashen is also critical of the National Reading Panel's
findings:

The NRP report missed a number of important studies. In The Power of Reading, *I found nine studies which lasted longer than one year; sustained silent reading was a winner in eight of them, and in one there was no difference. The NRP did not cite any of these studies, even though some appeared in very important, widely read journals. Some spectacular omissions include Elley and Mangubhai's Fiji study, published in the* Reading Research Quarterly *(1983), and Elley's Singapore study, in* Language Learning *(1991). The latter contains a review of several other successful SSR studies that the NRP failed to mention.* (2000)

SSR is necessary to allow students an opportunity to build their prior knowledge and background. Students who do not develop the habit of reading books, newspapers, and magazines end up as seniors in high school wondering why they have never heard of a guy named Al Qaeda. They become the ninth graders in my class who cannot tell me the name of the vice president of the United States. They become the native-speaking student in my high school class who highlighted the following words in a handout as words he did not understand: *lethal, ballot, backlash, via, barricade, ambitious, formidable,* and *abstain.* It's scary when a teenager doesn't understand the word *abstain,* wouldn't you say?

When it comes to vocabulary acquisition, SSR provides the best investment of reading time. As Krashen (1993b) notes:

✖ Each time an unfamiliar word is seen in print, a small increase in word knowledge typically occurs (8).
✖ Students who read a novel with many unique words actually learned the meaning of those words from context clues only (10).
✖ FVR results in better reading comprehension, writing style, vocabulary, spelling, and grammatical development (12).

The stakes are high. If those students who enter schools linguistically impoverished—thirty-two million words behind—do not read extensively, they will never catch up. This bears repeating: struggling readers who do not read voraciously will never catch up.

Students with the broadest vocabularies, of course, stand the greatest chance of scoring well on exams that measure vocabulary and comprehension. Unfortunately, a 2007 global study found that fourth-grade students in the United States, despite the emphasis on reading under No Child Left Behind, have actually lost ground in reading ability compared with students from around the world (Zuckerbrod 2007). This loss occurred between 2001 and

2006, years that, not surprisingly, coincide with the implementation of the No Child Left Behind Act.

Finland recently finished first in an international study of literacy. Finland has no standardized testing; yet, they produce the strongest readers in the world. Yes, I know the Finns are a more culturally homogeneous population than those students we find in our classrooms, but this should not minimize their ranking (after all, they finished ahead of all other homogeneous populations as well).

These findings remind me of the words of Lev Vygotsky, who said, "Children grow into the intellectual life of those around them" (1978, 88).

SSR provides many students with their only opportunity to develop a recreational reading habit. When I was in college, I waited tables at a restaurant that specialized in spaghetti. Though their menu has broadened over the years, when I worked there, spaghetti (with various sauces) pretty much made up the menu. As a poor college student, I often took advantage of the employee free meal program. The good news was I received a free plate of spaghetti before clocking in to work each night. The bad news was I received a free plate of spaghetti before clocking in to work each night. Though the spaghetti was good, it did not take long before I started seeing spaghetti in my nightmares. By the time I left that job, I was so sick of spaghetti I did not eat it again for years.

I think of the awfulness of eating spaghetti every night when I witness students who have progressed through the school system who are fed a steady diet of academic reading only. By the time they walk into my ninth-grade class, they have become sick of reading. I would tire of reading too if I was only encouraged to read difficult classics. I am not arguing against teaching classic literature. There is a real value in challenging students with longer, difficult texts (more on this in Chapters 3 and 4). However, when academic reading is the only kind of reading put on our students' plates, readicide occurs. As much as I love Dickens and Shakespeare, I would turn off to reading if I didn't have a balanced reading diet that included Scott Turow or Michael Connelly.

SSR has failed in a number of schools. In most cases of failure, one or more of the following were contributing factors:

✖ Students were placed in SSR without interesting books to read. Telling a student that reading is a worthwhile activity is one thing, having numerous interesting books for the student to choose from is another.
✖ Students were required (or allowed) to do academic reading or homework during SSR.

✖　Teachers did not understand the value of SSR. Often they were not reading with their students or were using this time to grade essays, catch up on paperwork, or answer emails.

To become a lifelong reader, one has to do a lot of varied and interesting reading. If students don't read much at home, school becomes the only place where "lighter" reading can take hold. When schools deprive students of the pleasures of recreational reading, we end up graduating test-takers who may never again read for pleasure.

Author Joel Epstein once said, "We are what we read" (1985, 395). True, but consider the flip side, "We are what we don't read." And when a student doesn't read, he turns into the eighteen-year-old in my third period who didn't vote because he didn't know what the word *proposition* on the ballot meant.

What You Can Do to Prevent Readicide

This chapter has made the point that readicide is occurring because our students are denied the varied authentic reading experiences foundational to building adolescent readers. Specifically, I discussed three negative trends in our schools:

1.　There is a dearth of interesting reading materials in our schools.
2.　Many schools have removed novels and other longer challenging works to provide teachers and students with more test preparation time.
3.　Students are not doing enough reading in school.

Let's now examine each of these individually in an effort to explore what you can do to turn the tide of readicide.

There Is a Dearth of Interesting Reading Materials in Our Schools

What you can do:

Take a stand. It is amazing how many teachers across this country have told me they do not have enough copies of a novel for students to take home and read. I am often told there are enough books for a class set but not enough books for each student to take an individual copy home. Therefore, all reading of the novel is done in class. What is also amazing to me is how many teachers have come to accept this situation.

I know that as teachers, we are faced with numerous battles. I also know that the there is much wisdom in the advice that we must choose our battles. If we fight every battle, we will suffer a collapse worse than the 2007 New York Mets. Let me be unequivocal: making sure every student has a book to take home to read is the single most important issue in our quest to develop young readers.

If students don't have books, they will never develop into readers. If students only read in school, they will never become lifelong readers. In fact, I contend that teachers whose students read only in school ensure that their students will forever remain behind grade level as readers. Harsh words? Yes. But a system that does not provide books for students to take home to read is an immoral system, and teachers who quietly resign themselves to these systems contribute to the problem.

I can already hear some of you shouting at me, particularly those of you who teach in financially strapped schools: "My school doesn't have money for books!" or "I have asked, but my principal says we have to make do with what we have!" I would counter these real concerns with what I know: your school district does have money. That's not the problem. The problem is where districts allocate their resources. If your students don't have books, your school district is spending its money in the wrong places. (Here is something else I know: many districts often squander large sums of money. My own district recently required fifty teachers to attend a test-taking strategy seminar. Total cost: $20,000. Total benefit: almost zero.) If your students do not have books, your school district's priorities are misplaced.

Again, I can hear your concerns: "But I am a teacher, not an administrator!" True, but when the decisions upstairs play a role in permanently damaging the literacy development of our children, it is time for us to take a stand. If you need books, go to your department chair. If your department chair says there is no funding for books, go to your principal. If your principal says there is no money for books, go to the director of instructional services. If the director of instructional services says there is no money for books, go to the assistant superintendent. If the assistant superintendent says there is no money for books, go to the superintendent. If the superintendent says there is no money for books, go to the school board. If the school board says there is no money for books, go to the media, go to local businesses, go to the community. Make a stink. Make it happen. Of all the battles we face, this is the one worth falling on your sword for. If none of the above steps work, go teach somewhere else. No one should consciously be part of a system that ensures that kids fail. That's unconscionable.

Augment books with authentic, real-world text. In *Proust and the Squid,* Maryanne Wolf (2007) discusses the importance of producing "bi-textual" readers—students who garner reading from a number of different sources. To help facilitate this, teachers need to augment the curriculum by surrounding the core curriculum with as much real-world text as possible.

When I realized that in two different class periods I did not have a single ninth-grade student who could identify the vice president of the United States, I grasped how serious the lack of my students' reading depth had become. Yes, they can recognize foreshadowing in *Lord of the Flies*, but they have little understanding of what is going on in the world outside of their high school. Sadly, they are light years away from being multitextual readers.

One way I addressed this problem in my classroom was by adding a weekly reading task I call "The Article-of-the-Week." These are real-world writings taken from straight news stories, essays, editorials, blogs, and speeches. I cull them from newspapers, magazines, and websites. Sometimes the articles are related to the unit we are currently studying and sometimes they are completely unrelated, but all the articles have one purpose—to broaden my students' knowledge of the world. This past school year, for example, my students read and studied more than thirty different articles (see Figure 2.2).

9/11 suspects may face death penalty
Our schools are facing drastic budget cuts
1 in 100 Americans are now in prison
The environmental hazards posed by bottled water
A proposal to tax junk food
Inside a Chicago street gang
The ten greatest inventions of all time
Gambler sues casino to recoup her losses
An editorial on California's decision to legalize gay marriage
The soldier whose job it is to inform families they have lost a loved one
Global warming
The One Laptop per Child Project
New health care clinics are opening inside traditional businesses
How the American Disabilities Act affects health care
The pervasiveness of photography that has been airbrushed

Children of baby boomers are flooding colleges with applications
Rethinking nuclear power
The Texas polygamy story
Cyclone kills hundreds in Myanmar
Hope fades in search for China earthquake victims
The influence the next president will have in selecting Supreme Court members
An account of a firefight in Iraq
Violations of "Islamic teachings" take toll on Iraqi women
The Iraq money pit
An overview of global poverty
Cocaine-addiction vaccine is in the works
How Starbucks is changing music distribution
Fear-based ads sneak into subconscious, researcher says
The NSA—America's most secret agency
Are Americans overmedicated?
A number of articles on both the Republican and Democratic primaries

FIGURE 2.2
ARTICLE-OF-THE-WEEK TOPICS FOR THE 2007–2008 SCHOOL YEAR

Per: 2
AoW 9.8.08

Directions:
1. Demonstrate evidence of close reading.
2. Highlight your confusion.
3. Answer the two questions at the bottom of the page.
4. Write a 1+ page reflection in your WN.

Do Cell Phones Cause Cancer?

New doubt about what?

Are cell phones dangerous?

The scientific consensus has long been that they are not—though recently, some troubling research has led to new doubts. As soon as mobile phones began hitting the market in the 1980s, concerns were raised that the electromagnetic radio waves they emit might cause brain tumors and other types of cancer. But as cell phones became ubiquitous, at least a dozen major studies found no such link. The Food and Drug Administration said recently that three large epidemiological studies since 2000 showed "no harmful effects" from cell phone use, and the World Health Organization holds a similar view. The theory that cell phones pose health risks, says Dr. Eugene Flamm, chairman of neurosurgery at New York's Montefiore Medical Center, "defies credulity."

Common Place

How do they really know that cell phones don't put people at risk? Some effects can be long-term and dormant for a period of time.

goes against their credibility. doesn't make sense

What's the basis of that contention?

Cell phones emit non-ionizing radiation, waves of energy that are too weak to break the chemical bonds within cells or to cause the DNA damage known to cause cancer. There is simply no known biological mechanism to explain how non-ionizing radiation might lead to cancer. But some researchers say that the lack of a known mechanism does not rule out the possibility that one exists and has yet to be understood. They also say that older studies on cell phone safety contained a major flaw.

Like the researchers say, just because something is unknown to society doesn't mean it's not there.

what was the flaw?

What's the flaw?

As the FDA itself acknowledges, most of the studies examined cell phone use over a period of about three years—not long enough to rule out the possibility of long-term effects. "It takes at least 10, 20, or 30 years to see exposure to cancer," says Israeli neuroscientist Dr. Siegal Sadetzki. She points out that it took decades before scientists could prove that people exposed to radiation at Hiroshima had a much higher incidence of brain tumors. Critics also say that the studies have largely ignored the impact of cell phones on teenagers and preteens, whose developing brains may be more vulnerable, especially since many of them tend to use cell phones for hours every day (see box).

Scientists ignore the impact on teenagers? why? Can't they see that it's mainly the teenagers who are addicted to their cell phones? It's practically glued to their ear.

What does recent research show?

Two major studies have found an association, though not a causal relationship, between cell phone use and certain cancers. Last year, the American Journal of Epidemiology published data from Israel finding a 50 percent higher risk of cancer of the parotid, a salivary gland near the ear, among habitual cell phone users. A Swedish analysis of 16 studies in the journal Occupational and Environmental Medicine showed a doubling of risk for acoustic neuroma, a tumor that occurs where the ear meets the brain, after 10 years of heavy cell phone use. "There are some very disconcerting findings that suggest a problem," says Dr. Louis Slesin, editor of Microwave News, an industry publication that tracks the research, "although it's much too early to reach a conclusive view."

How long does someone have to use a phone to get cancer on their salivary gland? How do they know that it came from cell phone use?

(not AAAW. doesn't start the sentence)

What does the industry say?

Citing the authority of the World Health Organization, cell phone companies say the technology poses no known risks and requires no precautions. They also stress that

FIGURE 2.3
ARTICLE-OF-THE-WEEK EXAMPLE (ANNOTATED)

The Article-of-the-Week (AoW) is distributed every Monday and collected every Friday. (See Figure 2.3 for an example.) Since starting this weekly assignment, the entire English Department at my school has gotten behind the idea. That means every student at Magnolia High School receives an AoW. Teachers take turns selecting the articles, and a different article is distributed at each grade

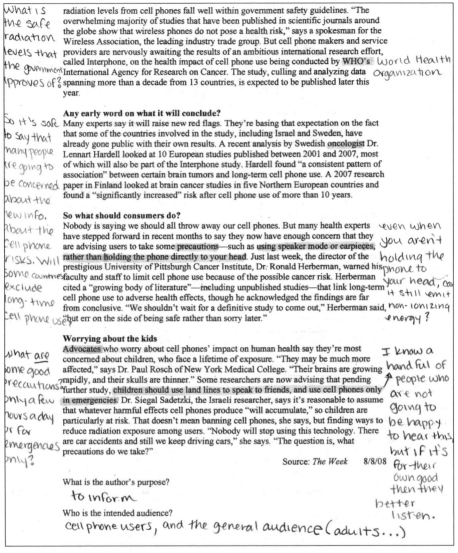

[Handwritten margin annotations, left side:]
What is the safe radiation levels that the government approves of?

So it's safe to say that many people are going to be concerned about the new info. About the cell phone risks. Will some countries exclude long-time cell phone use?

what are some good precautions? only a few hours a day or for emergencies only?

[Typeset article text:]

radiation levels from cell phones fall well within government safety guidelines. "The overwhelming majority of studies that have been published in scientific journals around the globe show that wireless phones do not pose a health risk," says a spokesman for the Wireless Association, the leading industry trade group. But cell phone makers and service providers are nervously awaiting the results of an ambitious international research effort, called Interphone, on the health impact of cell phone use being conducted by WHO's International Agency for Research on Cancer. The study, culling and analyzing data spanning more than a decade from 13 countries, is expected to be published later this year.

[Handwritten, right margin:] World Health Organization

Any early word on what it will conclude?
Many experts say it will raise new red flags. They're basing that expectation on the fact that some of the countries involved in the study, including Israel and Sweden, have already gone public with their own results. A recent analysis by Swedish oncologist Dr. Lennart Hardell looked at 10 European studies published between 2001 and 2007, most of which will also be part of the Interphone studies. Hardell found "a consistent pattern of association" between certain brain tumors and long-term cell phone use. A 2007 research paper in Finland looked at brain cancer studies in five Northern European countries and found a "significantly increased" risk after cell phone use of more than 10 years.

So what should consumers do?
Nobody is saying we should all throw away our cell phones. But many health experts have stepped forward in recent months to say they now have enough concern that they are advising users to take some precautions—such as using speaker mode or earpieces, rather than holding the phone directly to your head. Just last week, the director of the prestigious University of Pittsburgh Cancer Institute, Dr. Ronald Herberman, warned his faculty and staff to limit cell phone use because of the possible cancer risk. Herberman cited a "growing body of literature"—including unpublished studies—that link long-term cell phone use to adverse health effects, though he acknowledged the findings are far from conclusive. "We shouldn't wait for a definitive study to come out," Herberman said, "but err on the side of being safe rather than sorry later."

[Handwritten, right margin:] even when you aren't holding the phone to your head, can it still emit non-ionizing energy?

Worrying about the kids
Advocates who worry about cell phones' impact on human health say they're most concerned about children, who face a lifetime of exposure. "They may be much more affected," says Dr. Paul Rosch of New York Medical College. "Their brains are growing rapidly, and their skulls are thinner." Some researchers are now advising that pending further study, children should use land lines to speak to friends, and use cell phones only in emergencies. Dr. Siegal Sadetzki, the Israeli researcher, says it's reasonable to assume that whatever harmful effects cell phones produce "will accumulate," so children are particularly at risk. That doesn't mean banning cell phones, she says, but finding ways to reduce radiation exposure among users. "Nobody will stop using this technology. There are car accidents and still we keep driving cars," she says. "The question is, what precautions do we take?"

Source: *The Week*   8/8/08

[Handwritten, right margin:] I know a handful of people who are not going to be happy to hear this, but if it's for their own good then they better listen.

What is the author's purpose?
to inform

Who is the intended audience?
cell phone users, and the general audience (adults...)

FIGURE 2.3
ARTICLE-OF-THE-WEEK EXAMPLE (ANNOTATED) *(continued)*

level. (You may access the articles on my website, www.kellygallagher.org.) Students who stay at our school throughout their high school years will graduate having read approximately 140 articles. (Remember, these articles are in addition to the standard curriculum.) Reading 140 real-world articles builds our students' knowledge capital so that when they graduate they will have a better chance of comprehending our world. They will know who al Qaeda is. They will recognize the vice president of the United States. They will be dialed into the real world.

I will discuss how students interact with the AoWs and how I assess them in Chapter 4.

If you want to find out how little your students know about the world, hand them a copy of *Newsweek*. Paging through the articles with students is a sobering experience. When I realized that their lack of knowledge was seriously hindering their understanding of real-world issues, I augmented my curriculum with one class set of *Newsweek* delivered to my classroom each week. I didn't have the money to fund this program, so I went up the hierarchy of decision-makers until someone "found" the money to pay for a class set subscription. One night a week, students take the magazine home to read. First period gets Monday night, second period gets Tuesday night, and so on. Sometimes I choose an article as the focus of their reading; other times students are free to pick an article to read. Much like the AoW, this reading is done in addition to the standard curriculum.

Here are some assignments I have given my students for overnight *Newsweek* reading:

- ✖ Choose your three favorite quotes or passages from this week's issue and write a reflection for each in your writer's notebook.
- ✖ Write down five things you learned by reading this week's issue. Which of these five do you think is the most important to know? Explain.
- ✖ Which article in the magazine do you think is least newsworthy? Why do you think the magazine ran the article? Defend your answers.
- ✖ After reading an interesting article, create a t-chart. On the left side, bullet the key points of the article. On the right side, list what the article doesn't say. What has been left out?
- ✖ Which photograph in this week's issue is most effective? Explain why you chose this photograph.
- ✖ After reading this article, reflect on the author's purpose and who the intended audience might be.
- ✖ Choose an article that may contain bias. Identify the bias and explain the "other side."
- ✖ Pick three articles and rewrite their headlines. Explain why your headlines are better.
- ✖ Free response. Respond to an article of your choice any way you see fit.

Newsweek has proved to be an invaluable student source for real-world text. I am determined that my students will not only pass the state tests, but that they will leave my classroom with a much greater understanding of the world.

Be the "discussion director" on your campus. Many of you know Harvey Daniels's *Literature Circles* (2002), in which students are assigned roles to help facilitate collaborative thought. One of these roles is the "discussion director," whose job is to make sure the group stays on task and doesn't stray from its focus. With this role in mind, I suggest that you become a discussion director among your faculty, working to keep the faculty's focus on surrounding students with real-world text across the curriculum.

Many teachers have become so buried by the pressures of teaching to the test and by the overburdening number of standards that they have lost sight of the value of students reading newspapers, magazines, Internet articles, blogs, and other valuable sources of information. Instead, teachers are wed to their textbooks in a solemn march to get to the exams. However, most teachers genuinely want to do what's best for their students. These teachers are not intentionally harming kids; they have simply forgotten the importance of surrounding their students with interesting real-world reading.

Someone on your campus needs to be the discussion director—someone who raises this issue and keeps your faculty focused. Do your students have access to interesting books? Do they have time to read? It all starts with raising the awareness level of the faculty and administrators. To bolster your argument, it is helpful to share research. I have found the following research articles to be good places to start:

✖ http://edresearch.info/by_children.asp
✖ http://www.readingrockets.org/article/394
✖ http://www.aft.org/pubs-reports/american_educator/spring2003/AE_SPRNG.pdf
✖ http://www.sdcoe.k12.ca.us/score/promising/tips/tipfvr.html
✖ http://www.sdkrashen.com/articles/pac5/all.html

Once awareness is raised, be the torchbearer on this issue. Do not allow the faculty's attention to stray. Ask your administrators to keep this issue in focus. At my school, I ask for five minutes whenever we have a teacher-only day or a late-start day. I use this time to remind my colleagues of the importance of SSR and why bringing authentic text into the classroom is a priority.

Establish a book flood zone. Warrick Elley, the New Zealand researcher, studied the reading achievement of more than 200,000 students in thirty-two countries and found a strong correlation between time spent reading and reading achievement (1991). Not surprisingly, he also found that the amount of a student's out-of-school reading strongly relates to reading achievement levels. A study by the National Assessment of Educational Progress (NAEP) came to a similar conclusion. It found "that students who read for fun almost every day outside of school scored higher on the NAEP assessment of reading achievement than children who read for fun only once or twice a week, who in turn outscored children who read for fun outside of school only once or twice a month, who in turn, outscored children who hardly ever or never read for fun outside of school" (EdResearch.info).

Notice the key phrase in the NAEP study: "read for fun." Not reading to analyze the author's use of tone. Not reading to answer multiple-choice questions. Reading for fun. If students are to read for fun, they need fun books to read. Many of them. They need immersion in a book flood, and because many of our students come from print-poor environments at home, that book flood needs to be found at school.

I have found that placing students in a daily book flood zone produces much more reading than occasionally taking them to the library. Consider, for example, Lois Duncan, the author of *I Know What You Did Last Summer* and other murder mysteries. Chillingly, in the middle of writing all these murder mysteries, Duncan's own teenage daughter, Kaitlyn, was murdered. The authorities never captured the killer or killers, which led Duncan to write *Who Killed My Daughter?* I was stunned when I read this book, so I couldn't wait to tell my students about it. The conversation went something like this:

Mr. Gallagher: I read a book last night I know many of you will enjoy.
Students: (Silence.)
Mr. Gallagher: How many of you have seen *I Know What You Did Last Summer*?
Students: (Many hands shoot up.)
Mr. Gallagher: This is creepy, but did you know that in real life—in the middle of writing a number of murder mysteries—that the author who wrote that book had a teenage daughter who was murdered? Worse, the police never found the murderer, so the author, Lois Duncan, wrote a work of nonfiction titled *Who Killed My Daughter?*
Students: (Silence . . . but showing some signs of being mildly interested.)
Mr. Gallagher: Because I like this book so much, I checked our school library this morning and found it has three copies. I give this book a strong recom-

mendation and suggest you get to the library after school ASAP to snag one of the copies.

I gave this speech to every one of my classes, 165 students. After school, I stopped in the library and was chagrined to see two of the three copies of the book still sitting on the shelf. Apparently, my speech had motivated exactly one of my students to walk from my room to the library to check out the book.

Unhappy with that result, I checked out the other two copies of *Who Killed My Daughter?* and brought them to class the next day. The conversation that day went something like this:

Mr. Gallagher: I noticed only one student checked out the book I recommended yesterday, *Who Killed My Daughter?* That's too bad because I really think many of you will like this book. In fact, let me give you a taste of the book by reading the first few paragraphs (I read):

> *Our teenage daughter Kaitlyn was chased down and shot to death while driving home from a girlfriend's house on a peaceful Sunday evening.*
>
> *Police dubbed the shooting "random."*
>
> *"You're going to have to accept the fact that the reason Kait died was because she was in the wrong place at the wrong time," they told us.*
>
> *But to our family the circumstances did not add up to "random," especially after we made the shocking discovery that Kait had been keeping some very dangerous secrets from us"* (7).

(Pause.) Now . . . who is interested in reading this book?

Students: (A number of hands are raised.)

Mr. Gallagher: Okay, because I saw their hands first, I will give my two copies to Alex and Kristi. I will put everyone else on a waiting list.

I then created a waiting list for the book—the same book my students wouldn't walk thirty-eight steps from my classroom to the school library to pick up, a book that will get passed to numerous students throughout the school year. What did I learn from this experience? Instead of always taking students to the library, it is often much more effective to bring the library to the students. Having the Lois Duncan book in the classroom made a big difference. There is something powerful about surrounding kids with interesting books (see Appendix A for a list of books my students love to read). I have 2,000 books in my room, and because of this, my students do a lot more reading. Establishing a book flood is probably the single most important thing I have done in my teaching career.

It also helps to remember that building a classroom library is a career-long pursuit. Unfortunately, so is finding the funding sources to buy books. Though I mention these in my first book, *Reading Reasons* (2003), it may be worthwhile to mention the funding sources that may be available on your campus:

* Principal's discretionary funds
* Title I money
* Title II money
* School improvement funds
* One-time money
* Grant money
* Curriculum cycle money

Other ways to bring books into your classroom:

Organize book drives. At the end of the year, I conduct a book drive in my classes. I ask graduating seniors to donate a book to my classroom library as a way of leaving a literary footprint behind. I ask them to consider the best book they have read and to donate a copy of it, new or used. Every year, this generates a couple of hundred of books for my classroom library (many students donate more than one title).

Order books from Scholastic.com. I loved getting those monthly book order forms in school when I was a student. Once a month I distribute the order forms to my students, and every time they order a book I receive points toward free books. Scholastic also has large warehouses across the country, and many of them conduct a once-a-year massive sale. See their website for details.

Solicit donations at Back-to-School Night. Appendix A lists books that even my most reluctant readers enjoy reading (this is an updated list from the book lists found in *Reading Reasons*). Copy this list and send it home before Back-to-School Night with a brief letter asking parents to donate a title or two when they visit. This creates two benefits: your classroom library grows, and it presents an opportunity at Back-to-School Night to discuss with parents the importance of establishing a book flood.

Discover used books on Amazon.com. I budget $50 a month to augment my classroom library, and much of it is used to purchase used books at Amazon.com, where you can buy excellent books for as little as a penny. That's the good news.

The bad news is shipping is usually $3, but even with shipping factored in, it is still an inexpensive way to build a classroom library.

Recognize and fight against summer reading loss. It seems almost silly to establish a book flood zone for part of the year, only to let our students out for three months of summer vacation. Studies have shown that many students lose ground in the summer months, particularly those students from print-poor home environments. Anne McGill-Franzen and Richard Allington (2004) note the following:

✖ Summer reading loss is one factor contributing to the achievement gap between more and less economically advantaged students (1).

✖ Children from low-income families have more restrictive access to books, both in school and at home, than their more advantaged peers (1).

✖ Lower-achieving readers read less in school and out of school than higher-achieving readers. Evidence points to a social-class effect here, with poor children having fewer reading opportunities (1).

✖ Better readers read more than poorer readers, supporting the importance of extensive, successful reading experiences in the development of reading proficiency (1).

McGill-Franzen and Allington (2004) also note that summer vacations, on average, "create an annual reading achievement gap of about three months between students from middle- and lower-class families . . . In other words, the reading achievement of children from low-income families declined between June and September while the achievement of more economically advantaged children remain stable or inched upward" (2). The result? By the end of the sixth grade, summer reading loss alone creates a reading gap of eighteen months.

If we are serious about preventing summer reading loss, then we have to get serious about discussing how to motivate our students to read over the summer. One research study suggests that summer reading loss can be prevented if students read four to five books over the summer (Kim 2004). With this in mind, isn't it interesting that many school systems require students in the honors track to read over the summer, but often do not have any summer reading expectations for students in the nonhonors tracks? The irony, of course, is that the nonhonors students are the students who most need summer reading. Why should we have high expectations only for advanced students, while less-proficient readers fall farther behind each summer?

The truth is that all students should be required to read in the summer. For example, I taught two ninth-grade classes last year, and it was arranged so that they would be my students again in the tenth grade. Because they would be returning to me after the summer, I was able to establish summer reading expectations. My students are assigned two high-interest books to read over the summer. One book, Victor Villaseñor's *Rain of Gold*, is chosen by me; the other is self-selected and is recreational in nature. If my students do not read over the summer, they will continue falling behind. We have to get creative in ways to prevent summer reading loss from occurring, and the scheduling of students with the same teacher for two years is one way to address this critical problem.

A final, but important, note about summer reading: though I agree with the honors-level philosophy of assigning required reading over the summer, and I agree that all students should be required to read over the summer, I disagree strongly about the types of summer reading assignments students are being asked to complete. Want to kill the love of reading in young readers? Then continue to assign *Hamlet* or *Great Expectations* for them to wrestle with on their own. Books such as *The Grapes of Wrath* should not be assigned during summer vacation, because reading these books without the guidance of a teacher becomes an exercise in frustration and futility for students. I have read *The Grapes of Wrath* three times, and each time I have discovered new thinking in it. Why would I expect a teenager to take it home and read it on her own for the first time?

Though we certainly want to develop academic readers, summer is not the time to do so. Instead, summer is the time when educators should be focused on developing recreational reading habits in young students. Summer is the time our students should be reading high-interest (and high-quality) fiction and nonfiction. Summer is the time our students should be curling up with *Tuesdays with Morrie* or *Fast Food Nation*. We should be putting high-interest, accessible books into their hands: *The Kite Runner*, not *Heart of Darkness*. Our goal should be to nurture young readers, not to kill them.

Many Schools Have Removed Novels and Other Longer Challenging Works to Provide Teachers and Students with More Test Preparation Time

Earlier in this chapter I discussed the dangers of eliminating longer, challenging works from the curriculum. With this in mind, here is what you can do to prevent readicide:

Challenge all students with difficult text. Teachers have a duty to challenge students with complex novels and longer works. We are English teachers, not English assigners, and as such, we are paid to get in our classroom and present texts that stretch our students' thinking. It is our job to work our students through text that is a little bit too hard for them. It's not the difficult novels that are the problem; it's how they are taught that is the problem. (Specific, effective strategies that challenge students with difficult text will be discussed in Chapters 3 and 4.)

Recognize the difference between liking a text and gleaning value from a text. Get over the notion of students liking the book. Before I teach *1984*, for example, I already know some of my students will like the novel and some of my students will not like the novel. Let's face it: some students are not going to like a dark, science fiction dystopia that ends with all humanity being snuffed out. Frankly, I don't really care if they like it. What I care about is that all my students see the value in reading *1984* and that the novel has a lot to say to the modern reader. As an adult, I am a different person because I have read *1984*. I see my government differently, I consider privacy issues differently, and I have a heightened sense of propaganda and language manipulation—all because I have read this novel. This is not the same as liking the novel. Students may or may not like the novel, but I want all of them to understand the value that comes from reading it—a value that will help them become smarter people long after they leave school.

Make sure teachers and administrators are aware of the damage done to adolescents when students' brains are not stretched by longer, challenging works. Remember Maryanne Wolf's (2007) warning that all adolescents go through key developmental brain stages and that when they are not stretched in these periods of life their cognitive windows run the risk of shutting down. Be the lead person on your campus and in your district in making sure that curricular decision-makers understand what is at stake—that a short, choppy curriculum can damage our students' ability to think long after they leave the K–12 school system. Share the research found on page 51 of this chapter. For additional support, share some of the excellent research found in David Sousa's *How the Brain Learns to Read* (2004), Patricia Wolfe's *Brain Matters: Translating Research into Classroom Practice* (2004), and Eric Jensen's *Teaching with the Brain in Mind* (2005).

Testing pressures aside, most administrators and teachers want to do what is in the best, long-term interest of kids. However, many of them are unaware of what brain research says about removing novels in favor of test preparation

materials. On behalf of your students, it may be up to you to raise the conscious-
ness of administrators.

Students Are Not Doing Enough Reading in School

What you can do:

**Conduct your own research to find out how much students are reading in
your school.** Recently, I asked my students to chart how much reading they
actually did in their classes as they worked through a typical school day. After a
six-hour school day, my freshman students read an average of seventeen minutes
in one school day; my seniors averaged thirteen minutes (these totals excluded
my English class). Interesting, but not surprising, was the finding that students
in the honors classes by far read the most. Students in the nonhonors tracks
(those who most need reading practice) read the least. This is in line with many
studies that have found that in a typical school day students aren't doing much
reading.

I am not sure that teachers from across the curriculum are aware of how little reading their students are actually doing. Make them aware. Conduct your
own study and share the results with your faculty. (I was careful not to ask for
teachers' names in my informal study.) Remind teachers that for many of our
students, school is the only place they'll have the opportunity to develop reading
skills. If our schools do not demand that our students get lots of reading practice (both academic and recreational reading experiences), they will not become
readers. Remind your peers that we are not simply content-area teachers. We are
all literacy teachers as well, and as such, it is a moral imperative that we provide
a setting in which tons of reading occurs. Piano players need to play a lot before
they become good piano players. Readers need to read a lot before they become
good readers. This should be nonnegotiable. Unfortunately, I have found that
schools have become such extremely busy places that authentic reading experiences are often buried under lectures, group work, films, worksheets, and test
preparation. Raising your faculty's awareness of this problem is the first step in
addressing the lack of reading occurring on campus.

Avoiding the Tsunami

Mem Fox, celebrated children's author, once told me a story about her daughter, Chloe, a native Australian, who came home distraught one day from an American elementary school.

"What's the matter, Chloe?" Mem asked.

"I had a bad day in school," she replied. "I wish I were back in Australia." Chloe went on to explain to her mother about how reading time was ruined by the teacher's insistence on repeatedly stopping so that students could analyze the book.

"Why do you wish you were back in Australia?" Mem asked.

"Because if I were in Australia," Chloe replied, "I could have read four books by now."

Chloe's lament encapsulates what has gone wrong in our schools: the creation of readicide through intensive overanalysis of literature and nonfiction. Young readers are drowning in a sea of sticky notes, marginalia, and double-entry journals, and as a result, their love of reading is being killed in the one place where the nourishment of a reading habit should be occurring—in school. The irony, of course, is that as a young reader, Chloe was turned off to reading by the very teachers whose purpose was to turn her on to reading. Her love of reading, however, was squashed by the constant overteaching, the constant teacher-induced interruptions, the constant chopping up of great books. (When

Chloe made it to college, she decided to avoid English as a major because, in her words, "I couldn't bear to have books ruined for another three years." Fortunately, Chloe remained a reader despite the damaging approach of her teacher, but then again, it probably helped more than a little bit to have Mem Fox as her mother.)

There are many Chloes out there—young, developing readers who are being led to readicide by the overteaching of books in our schools. How does overteaching books lead to readicide? Specifically, the overanalysis of books

✖ prevents our students from experiencing the place where all serious readers want to be—the reading flow.
✖ creates instruction that values the trivial at the expense of the meaningful.
✖ spills over and damages our students' chances of developing recreational reading habits.

Let's take a closer look at each of these factors before discussing what we can do to offset the damage that happens when overteaching occurs.

Readicide Factor: The Overteaching of Books Prevents Our Students from Experiencing the Place Where All Serious Readers Want to Be—The Reading Flow

I live in Southern California, and one Friday after school, I flew to Michigan to participate in a reading conference. Because I had taught all week I was exhausted, and when I got on the plane, I pulled out our faculty book club selection, *Come Back*, a searing memoir recounting a mother's frantic efforts to save her teenage daughter from drug addiction. My plan was to read for a few minutes before catching up on some sleep. Four hours later, when I touched down in Detroit, I was still reading the book, completely engrossed. I had no recollection of taking off. I had no recollection of the flight. I had no recollection of who was sitting next to me, or of being asked by the flight attendant whether I wanted a drink. I had no recollection of landing. Four hours later, I finished that book as the plane was taxiing to the gate, lost in its pages, completely oblivious to the world around me. I had entered the reading flow—the place all experienced readers have come to know and cherish.

The "flow" that I experienced in reading *Come Back,* and the flow I want my students to experience in their reading lives, was first described by Mihaly Csikszentmihalyi (1990) in *Flow: The Psychology of Optimal Experience.* Csikszentmihalyi describes the flow as "the state in which people are so involved in an activity that nothing else seems to matter; the experience itself is so enjoyable that people will do it even at great cost, for the sheer sake of doing it" (1990, 4). The flow is where we want all our students to be when they read, the place Nancie Atwell, in *The Reading Zone,* describes as that place where young readers have to "come up for air" (2007, 12). As a reader, you know what Atwell is talking about, but unfortunately, many of my students have no idea what it means to come up for air while reading. I often ask them, "Have you ever watched a movie that was so good you actually forgot for a moment that you were sitting in a movie theater?" Almost every student will admit to having that experience. But when I ask them, "Have you ever read a book that was so good that you actually forgot for a moment where you were?" The answer is always far less responsive. Though they have developed the ability to get lost in a film, it is a different story when it comes to print. Many have never experienced the thrill of becoming utterly lost within a book. They have never experienced reading flow.

Why is this? Could it be that the endless reading hoops placed in front of young readers to jump through are actually exacerbating the problem? After all, we don't have students stop the films they watch every five minutes so they can discuss foreshadowing, developing themes, and the director's tone. Could it be that our students are turning off to great books because teachers are chopping the books up so much that achieving reading flow is impossible? Would you stay in a movie theater if the projectionist stopped the film twenty-two times?

The Chop-Chop Curriculum

On my desk is a copy of the Los Angeles Unified School District's (2007) unit of study for teaching *To Kill a Mockingbird.* This study unit, a guide to teaching Harper Lee's timeless novel, contains overarching questions, chapter study questions, essay questions, vocabulary lessons, activities for specific chapters, guided reading lessons, directions for setting up a writer's notebook, literary analysis questions, collaborative activities, oral presentations, handouts, transparencies, displays, quizzes, and projects. It also comes with an almost incomprehensible unit guide (see Figure 3.1). This guide is 122 pages long—almost half the length of the actual novel!

Opening this guide, you will find a step-by-step approach for teaching the novel. It includes twenty detailed lessons—twenty ways to slice up the novel.

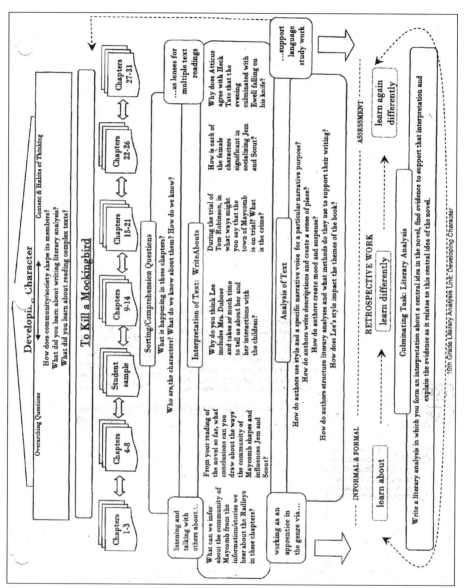

FIGURE 3.1
To Kill a Mockingbird UNIT GUIDE

Embedded in these twenty lessons are a bombardment of "goals" and "habits of thinking":

Goals

✖ *How community/society shapes its members through in-depth study and creation of complex interpretations of the novel through the unit's overarching inquiries (big ideas).*

✖ *Aspects of Harper Lee's style in writing* To Kill a Mockingbird, *including instances of subtle and direct word choice (diction), the narrator's voice, portrayals of motives and reactions of characters, and use of figurative language.*

✖ *Academic vocabulary in English language arts, focused on the terminology of literary criticism, which uses that vocabulary to have conversations that detect, comprehend, interpret, and evaluate relationships among ideas, characters, the narrator's voice, and the effect of the author's style on tone, mood, and theme.*

✖ *Detecting and comprehending the relationships among the novel's characters, including internal and external conflicts, motivations, influences, and how those relationships relate to the novel's plot lines.*

✖ *Characteristics of effective constructed literary analysis, focusing on their structures and techniques, and on assessing the appropriateness and quality of evidence and explanations.*

✖ *Vocabulary in the novel necessary to build literal and interpretive understandings within and across the novel's pages and chapters.*

✖ *Aesthetic qualities of Lee's style, such as dialogue, the impact of dialect, and flashbacks.*

Habits of Thinking

✖ *Find and use ways to remember, track, and retain information from a long and complex text such as this novel, over the course of several weeks.*

✖ *Inquire about the ideas and writing craft of this novel in order to engage with its ideas and characters, to develop one's own text-based interpretations, and to read critically to analyze aesthetic qualities of an author's style.*

✖ *Read a long and complex text multiple times for different purposes (getting the gist, interpreting, and analyzing) with different questions.*

✖ *Identify instances of complex text in passages, sentences, and/or vocabulary to be able to say why each instance of the text is complex, and then to be able to work individually and/or with the teacher and peers to untangle the text complexities.*

✖ *Read, write, and talk to "try out" and develop ideas and then to revisit them in later writing, reading, and talking.*

✖ *Plan, draft, develop, structure, revise, and evaluate literary analyses by studying models, engaging in conversations with peers and the teacher, and our own independent work.*

✖ *Use English language arts academic vocabulary, focused on the terminology of literary criticism, to begin to talk, think and write in ways that literary critics would talk, think, and write about a novel and other literary texts*

✖ *Reflect on how reading and writing changes how readers think, read, and write.*

✖ *Reflect on learning and what ways best support your learning.*

Culminating Assignment

✖ *How did class structure in Maycomb affect the events in the novel? Support your ideas, interpretations, and opinions with references to the text.*

✖ *How has Jem changed from the beginning of the book to the end of the book? Trace the ways the various characters and events in the novel contribute to his maturation. Support your ideas, interpretations, and opinions with references to the text.*

✖ *Trace the ways the various characters in the novel contribute to the socialization of either Jem or Scout. Support your ideas, interpretations, and opinions with references to the text.*

✖ *How community/society shapes its members through in-depth study and creation of complex interpretations of the novel through the unit's overarching inquiries (big ideas). The three "big ideas" for the unit: 1) How does community/society shape its members? 2) What did you learn about literary analysis? 3) What did you learn about reading complex texts?*

✖ *Aspects of Harper Lee's style in writing . . .*

Individually, each of the "goals" and "habits of thinking" is worthwhile. Collectively, however, they create a tsunami that drowns adolescent readers. This curricular guide, as thorough as it is, suffers from what I call the All Things in All Books Syndrome—the attempt to use one novel to pound dozens of different standards into the heads of our students. I understand why the Los Angeles Unified School District is promoting this approach. They are being held accountable to an impossible number of standards.

I am not suggesting that the goals of this unit are not worthy; they are. But teaching all of these lessons while students work through one novel is a recipe for readicide. If I were to follow this curricular guide step-by-step in my classroom, there is little doubt my students would exit my class hating *To Kill a Mockingbird* forever. Worse, students who have been taught to hate *To Kill a Mockingbird* will find themselves much farther down the road toward hating all reading. Is this the price we want to pay to exact higher test scores?

Remember Robert Marzano's (1998) comment that the biggest impediment to the teaching of standards is the overwhelming number of standards? There are too darn many of them. Any teacher who follows this unit of study will most certainly be playing a part in killing young readers. Of course, a terrible irony arises when one of the great books in American literature is used to turn students off to reading.

When I advocate structuring the reading experience so that students find the reading flow, it might help to make it clear what I am not advocating. I am not advocating that we give up teaching classic, difficult books. Students need the wisdom of these books now more than ever. I am not advocating that we stop requiring deeper analysis from our students. As I will argue in Chapter 4, our students need to sharpen their analytical skills. I am also not advocating that we allow students to self-select everything they read. If I did that, none of my students would read *Hamlet*. Every student should read *Hamlet*. What I am advocating is that we teachers must create reading situations in which our students discover the reading flow they need to achieve while reading both academic and recreational works, assigned and self-selected. Students who never experience reading flow are students who will never become readers.

Although I might be able to assign a book such as *Come Back* to a student and watch her achieve reading flow on her own, I am also painfully aware that I cannot hand most students *The Grapes of Wrath* or *1984* and sit back and watch them achieve reading flow. How we enable our students to achieve flow in an academic text requires a different set of teaching skills than those skills needed to help students discover flow in high-interest, recreational reading. I will detail how to help students read large chunks of academic text in Chapter 4; however, let me share what I know to be true: no student ever achieved reading flow from placing a blizzard of sticky notes in a book. No student ever achieved reading flow from using the same reading strategy ad infinitum. No student ever achieved reading flow from analyzing every nook and cranny of a complex work. Students in these reading situations are not coming up for air. They are coming up for life preservers.

Readicide Factor: The Overanalysis of Books Creates Instruction That Values the Trivial at the Expense of the Meaningful

In my first book, *Reading Reasons* (Gallagher 2003), I discuss the work of philosopher Kenneth Burke, who says the reason young people should read books is that it provides them with "imaginative rehearsals" for the real world. When children read books, Burke argues, they are not just reading stories. They are being given an opportunity to understand the complex world they live in (1968). Books enable adolescents to begin wrestling with those issues that remain universal in all our lives. Anne Frank's *Diary of a Young Girl* isn't just a recounting of the horrors of the Holocaust; reading her diary presents students with an opportunity to consider what is happening today in Darfur and other places in the world where genocide occurs. Reading *Animal Farm* is not simply an unusual trip to an English farm; Orwell's classic presents our students with the opportunity to discuss what happens when a citizenry fails to pay attention to its leadership. In an increasingly complex world, our students are in desperate need of these "rehearsals," and books are the perfect resource to foster this kind of thinking.

And this is what disturbs me when I read "tsunami" curricular guides: They direct teachers to chop up novels into so many pieces that novels are destroyed. Worse, they often gloss over, or ignore, the imaginative rehearsals these books offer. The real value in reading *To Kill a Mockingbird*, for example, is not so our students can "detect and comprehend the relationships among the novel's characters, including internal and external conflicts, motivations, influences, and how those relationships relate to the novel's plot lines" (Los Angeles Unified School District 2007, 2). It is not so our students can identify the "characteristics of effective constructed literary analysis, focusing on their structures and techniques, and on assessing the appropriateness and quality of evidence and explanations" (Los Angeles Unified School District 2007, 2). And it certainly is not so our students can "find and use ways to remember, track, and retain information from a long and complex text such as this novel, over the course of several weeks" (Los Angeles Unified School District 2007, 2). In fact, if your students are taking "several weeks" to read a single novel, which most assuredly will occur when you chop the novel into twenty lessons, readicide will most certainly occur.

I wonder what has happened to the imaginative rehearsals as I look at the 122-page teaching guide for *To Kill a Mockingbird*. The value in teaching this book is not simply to provide our students with a slice of cultural literacy or to teach them to recognize literary elements such as foreshadowing. The value comes when we use this great book as a springboard to examine issues in today's world. This opportunity seems to be largely missing in the district's mandated curriculum. A golden opportunity for our children to read, to write, and to debate about relevant issues is buried under 122 pages of mind-numbing instructions.

First, teaching *To Kill a Mockingbird* provides the modern student the opportunity to examine racism in their world. This is the imaginative rehearsal this book offers—to give our students a forum in which to examine racism in the world they are about to inherit. As I write this, numerous incidents regarding race invite closer examination from our students:

✖ Barack Obama, an African American man, has been elected president of the United States. Issues of race surrounded his candidacy, from inflammatory comments made by his former pastor, Reverend Jeremiah Wright, to accusations that both Senator Hillary Clinton, his Democratic primary opponent, and Republican members of John McCain's campaign played the race card. In addition, Pennsylvania governor Ed Rendell said there were voters in his state who were "not ready" to vote for a black man for president.

✖ Obama's campaign highlighted racial disparity in Congress:

	Percentage of the U.S. Population	U.S. House of Representatives 2007	U.S. Senate 2007	Presidents in U.S. History
African Americans	13%	8%	1%	0%
Asians and Pacific Islanders	5%	1.5%	2%	0%
Latinos	14%	5%	3%	0%
Native Americans	2%	0.2%	0%	0%
Whites	66%	85.3%	94%	100%

Source: www.anti-racismonline.org.

✖ In *Blink*, Malcolm Gladwell (2005) describes an experiment in which a group of people made up of blacks and whites were trained to negotiate buying a new car. The potential car buyers were all the same age, were all dressed the same, and were all instructed to present themselves as college-educated young professionals. After negotiating at 242 car dealerships in the Chicago area, the results were stunning. "The white men received initial offers from the salesmen that were $725 above the dealer's invoice (that is, what the dealer paid for the car from the manufacturer). White women got initial offers of $935 above invoice. Black women were quoted a price, on average, of $1,195 above invoice. And black men? Their initial offer was $1,695 above invoice" (93). Skin color (and gender) played a major part in determining what price was quoted to the potential car buyer.

✖ A wide gap exists in school funding. Because allocation of funds is often based on local property taxes, affluent schools generate more tax base. In California, for example, McKittrick Elementary School District in Kern County receives $33,325 per pupil—more than three times the state average of $9,061 per pupil. Beverly Hills schools receive $2,200 more per student than students in Manhattan Beach. Laguna Beach schools receive $13,367 per pupil, while neighboring Capistrano Valley receives $7,942. The list goes on, not only in California, but in schools across the country. I teach at a school, for example, with many poor students. My school's budget has run dry, and as a result, I have to buy copy paper at an office supply store with my own money. A few miles away is a school in an affluent area with so much money that its teachers can apply for any classroom need that arises. They are also able to provide many more curricular and extracurricular opportunities for their students. Unfortunately, as author Jonathan Kozol has noted in *The Shame of the Nation* (2006), schools in our country are still separate and unequal. Educational apartheid exists. Students of color are much more likely to attend poor schools.

✖ In the aftermath of Hurricane Katrina, a number of evacuees sought shelter in the Houston Astrodome. When asked about their plight, former First Lady Barbara Bush, in an interview on National Public Radio, responded, "What I'm hearing, which is sort of scary, is they all want to stay in Texas. Everyone is so overwhelmed by the hospitality. And so many of the people in the arena here, you know, were underprivileged anyway, so this is work-ing very well for them" (National Public Radio 2005). If one were to give Mrs. Bush the benefit of the doubt by saying her comments were not racist, a question still arises from her remarks: have we become a country where it is acceptable for people of color to be better off living in a baseball sta-dium–sized shelter than living in their own neighborhoods?

✖ Racial profiling still exists. In 2008, the Maryland state police settled a ten-year "Driving While Black" lawsuit stemming from a pattern of pulling over African American drivers on Interstate 95. In one survey, 77 percent of blacks felt that racial profiling was pervasive. In addition, 72 percent of African American male drivers felt they had been stopped because of their race (U.S. Department of Justice 2000). The Racial Profiling Data Collection Resource Center at Northeastern University shares numerous examples of racial profiling. For example, the New York City Police Department stopped a half-million pedestrians in 2006 for suspected criminal involvement. Of those stopped, 89 percent were nonwhites. In West Virginia, black drivers were one-and-a-half times more likely to be pulled over than white drivers. In Missouri, blacks were more likely to be searched when detained.

✖ Six black students at Jena High School in Central Louisiana, known as the Jena 6, were arrested after a school fight in which Justin Barker, a white student, was beaten, suffered a concussion, and sustained multiple bruises. Six black students were charged with attempted murder and conspiracy and faced up to 100 years in prison without parole. The fight took place amid mounting racial tension after a black student sat under a tree in the schoolyard where only white students sat. The next day nooses were found hanging from the tree. This case has sparked protests by those who see the arrests and charges as excessive and racially discriminatory. The protesters believed that white Jena youths involved were treated leniently.

Teaching *To Kill a Mockingbird* presents the teacher with an excellent opportunity to raise these issues, these imaginative rehearsals, in class. These themes found in the novel are universal. Reading and discussing Lee's novel enables students to make connections between the issues illustrated in the novel and the issues found in their world. It gives them the opportunity to read, to write, and to argue about these issues in a modern context. We do not want our students only to read stories; we want them to read novels to make them wiser about the world. We want to take advantage of the imaginative rehearsals that great literature provides before our students reach adulthood.

Strictly adhering to a 122-page curriculum guide will not make our students wiser about the world they are soon to inherit. Instead, it will achieve two things: It will (1) prepare them for the battery of state-mandated multiple-choice exams that loom in the spring and (2) ensure this classic novel is beaten to death. Worse, it will teach our students to hate reading, even when it comes to a great book like *To Kill a Mockingbird*.

I am not criticizing solely the Los Angeles Unified School District. I have run into this chop-chop approach in school districts across the country. Looking at this instructional guide, for example, reminds me of the teacher who approached me after a workshop in Virginia and asked whether I could offer her some feedback on a unit she was developing to teach *Romeo and Juliet*. She proceeded to show me how she had her students reach the deepest level of analysis by having them choose a key passage or word from each page in the play and then produce reflections in their reader's notebooks. One for each page. One hundred sixteen reflections—and she wondered why her students couldn't relate to the greatness of Shakespeare. Or the teacher in Pennsylvania who took her single favorite strategy from my book *Deeper Reading* (Gallagher 2004), applied it to everything she taught, and wondered why the students were bored to tears. Or the teacher on Amazon.com who, in giving *Deeper Reading* a five-star review, discusses how she took six months to teach one novel. Or the teacher in Texas who had the students place a sticky note reflection on every page of a novel— and wondered why her students were "near revolt" when it came time to read *My Brother Sam Is Dead.* Now imagine yourself sitting home, cozying up with a book you want to read. What would happen if I made you reflect after every page? How can a reader achieve any flow when stop signs are planted throughout the text? How fun would skiing be if you were required to stop every five feet and analyze your progress?

This chopping up of great writing to help prepare students for exams reminds me of one of my favorite Billy Collins (1996) poems:

Introduction to Poetry

I ask them to take a poem
and hold it up to the light
like a color slide

or press an ear against its hive.

I say drop a mouse into a poem
and watch him probe his way out,

or walk inside the poem's room
and feel the walls for a light switch.

I want them to waterski
across the surface of a poem
waving at the author's name on the shore.

But all they want to do
is tie the poem to a chair with rope
and torture a confession out of it.

They begin beating it with a hose
to find out what it really means.

Arming students with "rubber hoses" so they can flog literature might help them pass exams, but will this approach make our students avid readers? Will it prepare them for life beyond the exams? Should our students be spending all their time chopping up the novel? Or would their time be better spent developing reading flow, the kind of reading behavior we want them to adopt after graduation? Should they focus solely on the book, or use it as a springboard to understanding the world they are about to inherit? Do we really want to spend the bulk of our time, resources, and energy producing good test-takers who leave school not only ignorant but also hating reading?

Unfortunately, "flogging" novels has a worse secondary effect: it leaves the readers flogged, too.

Early in this chapter, I recounted getting lost in the book *Come Back* while I was on a cross-country flight. This memoir recounts a mother's desperate attempt to rescue her daughter from the ravages of drug abuse. One reason I was deeply drawn to the book was because I grew up with a sister who fought drug addiction throughout her life. Unlike the book, however, my sister's story did not end happily. Cathy eventually lost her battle with her addictions, dying at age 42.

Nine years later, as I read *Come Back*, I came across a passage that made me see the world differently. In this passage, the mother, Mia Fontaine, writes of the strained relationship she had with her mother. It seems her mother never told Mia she loved her:

> *I've spent so much time blaming and being angry at her for not telling me she loved me for forty years, I didn't see the most obvious thing, something that must have hurt her very much—that I waited forty years to tell her. Me, an expressive, modern woman, for whom saying I love you should have been no big deal, was mad at a woman who had no blueprint for things.* (Fontaine and Fontaine 2006, 246)

Fontaine recounts how her mother had been on her own since age 13, and how she had been forced into hiding from the Nazis at age 16. Her mother's upbringing clearly played a major role in her inability to say, "I love you." Once the author came to this realization, she was able to let go of years of bottled-up anger.

Sitting on the airplane reading this passage suddenly made it painfully clear that I had been holding in a tremendous amount of anger and resentment over my sister's death—an anger that had been pent up for years and had been misdirected at someone in my family. Touching down in Detroit, I realized my feelings were both wrong and destructive, and right then and there, I made a commitment to reconnect with this family member. Forgiveness was the higher road.

Of course, I knew this before reading *Come Back*. But reading this passage at this time and place in my life allowed something that was right in front of me to become visible. It provided me with a valuable imaginative rehearsal—a blueprint—for living a more productive life. Let me unequivocally say, however, that this epiphany never would have occurred had the flight attendant stopped at my seat every two minutes and made me place a sticky note on every page of the book. I might not have even made it to this significant passage on page 246 had I been asked to fill out numerous worksheets, to answer mind-numbing questions, or to spend the bulk of my reading time trying to "detect, comprehend, interpret, and evaluate relationships among ideas, characters, the narrator's voice, and the effect of the author's style on tone, mood, and theme" (Los Angeles Unified School District 2007, 2). These worksheets, quizzes, and literary analyses might prove valuable in building test-takers, but this focus on minutiae wrongly values the trivial at the expense of the meaningful. I am afraid the wisdom found in great books is getting drowned in the massive overemphasis of test preparation. When students read books solely through the lens of test preparation, they miss out on the opportunity to read books through the lens of life preparation. As a result, the imaginative rehearsals are lost, and when that happens, readicide sets in.

Readicide Factor: The Overteaching of Academic Texts Is Spilling Over and Damaging Our Students' Chances of Becoming Lifelong Readers

Think about that comforting place at home where you curl up with a good book. Mentally place yourself there. Now answer some brief questions. When you curl up with a book, do you do so with the idea of preparing for a state-mandated multiple-choice exam? Do you pause at the end of each chapter so you can spend an hour answering a worksheet filled with mind-numbing answers? Do you go to the library or bookstore to choose your next read so you can earn grades, candy, points, or other trivial external rewards? Do you finish your book quickly so you'll have more time to write a report, make a poster, or build a diorama? Do you begin reading with the hope this will be the book that will enable you to move up to a higher color level or higher point system?

These questions are so ridiculous they are rhetorical. As adult readers, we would not do any of these things. We would never buy a book at Barnes and

Noble if it came with mandated chapter-by-chapter exams. We would never read a book so that we could tackle worksheets afterward. We would never begin a new read with the expressed goal of earning points. And we would never feel compelled to read if we had to complete a project after every book. Yet, as teachers, we do all of these things to developing readers. We subject them repeatedly to treatments that are counterproductive to developing book lovers. And we do it book after book, year after year. Worse, we rationalize our behavior by believing we must prepare students to perform well at test time. Shameful.

Thinking about what we do to young readers reminds me of the time my students were reading recipe books and writing their own "recipes." Next time we do this assignment I will add the following:

The Kill-a-Reader Casserole

Take one large novel. Dice into as many pieces as possible.
Douse with sticky notes.
Remove book from oven every five minutes and insert worksheets.
Add more sticky notes.
Baste until novel is unrecognizable, far beyond well done.
Serve in choppy, bite-size chunks.

If we know our recipe is killing young readers, why do we keep following it?

What You Can Do to Prevent Readicide

If our students are to have any chance of discovering reading flow, if they are to have any chance to discover what it is like to come up for air while reading, if they are to have any chance of becoming lifelong readers, they will need what all readers need when they read: access to great books and large doses of uninterrupted time to read them. Writing this reminds me of a study conducted by Jeff McQuillan in *Teaching Reading in High School English Classes* (2001). McQuillan studied 240 Title I students at Anaheim High School who matched the overall demographics of the school at large: 92 percent Latino, half of them limited English proficient. The goal of the study group was simple: to increase the amount of time spent reading. Most of the adolescents who were chosen stated they rarely, if ever, read for pleasure and that they came from home environments where books were scarce.

Students chosen in this study were surrounded with high-interest books and given time to read them:

> The teachers started off slowly, allotting ten minutes a day during the first few weeks of the semester. Most students weren't accustomed to having time for pleasure reading in class, and some needed to work into the habit gradually. No other reading materials (e.g., textbooks) were allowed, and students were not permitted to work on homework or class assignments. Within four to six weeks, the time spent reading was gradually increased to fifteen and then twenty minutes. Several teachers noted that many students can sit, do nothing, and avoid reading for ten minutes, but when the SSR is twenty minutes, it is almost impossible for students to do nothing. At that point, they start reading. In some classes, students would read thirty minutes, complaining if they were given less time! Teachers report that 90 to 95 percent of their students were, in fact, reading their books, consistent with other reports that have found that, when properly implemented, almost all students take advantage of the SSR time provided. (McQuillan 2001, 75)

The results of McQuillan's study are telling. Though most students began the school year with a negative view of reading, by the end of the first semester, almost all of them had read several books on their own. In doing so, the students in the study showed statistically significant gains in writing fluency and writing complexity. McQuillan also found that the number of pages read was a significant predictor of student vocabulary gains, regardless of their previous vocabulary knowledge (2001).

It is important to note what the students in this study did not get. They didn't get worksheets. They didn't get points. They didn't get sticky notes to place in the books. They didn't get book report forms. They didn't get grades. They were simply given good books and time to read them.

Unfortunately, this is not the norm. On the contrary, it has become increasingly popular in school districts across the country to stick struggling or reluctant readers into packaged programs that reward students with points for reading books. Accelerated Reader (AR) is one such program. In AR, students are given mindless multiple-choice quizzes after they finish each book, and if they pass these quizzes, they are awarded points. Earn enough points and they progress to higher-level books in the program. In AR, the good news is that students read a lot of books. The bad news?

✖ Students can only read books found on the AR list. If a good book is not on the list, students are not allowed to read it.

✖ Students choose books for high point value, rather than for their level of interest.

✖ The reward system sends the message that the reason students should read is not to enjoy reading but to earn points. Students are taught to read for the wrong reasons.

✖ Chenowith (2001) found that although students did a significant amount of reading in the program, their reading dropped lower than nonparticipants within one month of exiting AR. Without the points, their motivation significantly decreased.

✖ Pavonetti, Brimmer, and Cipielewski (2002/2003) found that once students left AR they read on average ten hours a week less than nonparticipants. The program had short-term success but actually set young readers back in the long run.

Many teachers like Accelerated Reader and similar incentive-laden programs because they see students do a significant amount of reading. What they don't see is that programs such as AR and others that offer extrinsic rewards often lead to demotivating students after they have left the classroom.

Setting test scores aside for a moment, isn't it our overall, long-term goal to produce graduates who become lifelong readers? Isn't it paramount that students leave our schools seeing themselves as readers? What will be more important twenty years from now, that we have produced adults who remain avid readers? Or that we have produced adults who were once able to climb from level 3 to level 4 in a junior high school reading program?

With that in mind, let's return to McQuillan's (2001) study of reluctant readers at Anaheim High School. Recall that these students were immersed in a book flood and were simply given time to read. No tests. No worksheets. No points to earn. And while it is important to remember that these students showed significant gains in reading and writing, what is often overlooked is that this group exited the study liking reading. These students, most of whom expressed disdain for reading upon entering the study, discovered reading to be a worthwhile and rewarding pursuit. Sure, they made academic gains, but much more importantly, they began to see themselves as readers. They made this discovery without points being dangled in front of them. In fact, just the opposite seems to have occurred: it appears they came to this discovery because points were not dangled in front of them.

This is not a surprise. Numerous studies have found the most powerful motivator that schools can offer to build lifelong readers is to provide students with time in the school day for free and voluntary reading (FVR). Pilgreen and Krashen (1993) found that FVR is a strong indicator for the amount of reading students will do outside of school, and Greaney and Clarke (1975) found the effect appears to *last years after the SSR program ends.*

Unfortunately, testing pressure often trumps reason. Five years ago, all eighteen schools in my district provided SSR time so that students would have the opportunity to discover books and develop a reading habit. Today, in the shadow of high-stakes testing, my school is the last one that still provides time for free reading.

In this chapter, I contend that teachers are setting students on the road to readicide by overteaching books. In teaching academic texts, students are drowning in a sea of sticky notes, worksheets, and quizzes. As a result, the trivial is often highlighted at the expense of the meaningful. In addition, recreational reading is either tied to silly reward systems or is being removed altogether to make room for test preparation. Rather than building lifelong readers, these approaches are destroying the desire to read. What can we do about it? First, let's look at what we can do as we teach academic texts.

Teach Students to Recognize the Value That Comes from Reading Academic Texts

I have done many difficult things in my life. I have run a marathon. I have eaten escargot to impress a date. I have sat in the middle seat of a cross-country flight, wedged between a snorer and a person in desperate need of Gas-X. Worse, I have sat through *Sex and the City*. But all of these pale in comparison to the hardest thing I have ever done: stand in front of thirty-seven teenagers with the expressed purpose of teaching *Hamlet*. When I say thirty-seven teenagers, what I really mean is thirty-seven hormonal prehumans, who generally hate to read, who would rather talk about the game on Friday night, who have decided that since there is only a month to go before graduation that it's time to gear down, and who have decided it is their mission on this planet to complain anytime I suggest they read anything academic.

Despite all this, teenagers, like all people, are willing to work hard when they recognize that their efforts will bring them something valuable. Thus, a mistake teachers make when approaching difficult text is that they don't spend time teaching students the value that can come from serious reading. If I want my reluctant readers to take *Hamlet* seriously, for example, I must spend some time helping them to see the value of reading the text. Before reading the play, for example, I might share the famous advice scene between Polonius and his son, Laertes. In this scene, Laertes prepares to travel abroad to school. Before he departs, his father advises him on how to live a productive life:

And these few precepts in thy memory
See thou character. Give thy thoughts no tongue,
Nor any unproportion'd thought his act.   64
Be thou familiar, but by no means vulgar.
The friends thou hast, and their adoption tried,
Grapple them to thy soul with hoops of steel;
But do not dull thy palm with entertainment   68
Of each new-hatch'd, unfledg'd comrade. Beware
Of entrance to a quarrel; but being in,
Bear't that the opposed may beware of thee.
Give every man thine ear, but few thy voice;   72
Take each man's censure, but reserve thy judgment.
Costly thy habit as thy purse can buy,
But not express'd in fancy; rich, not gaudy;
For the apparel oft proclaims the man,   76
And they in France of the best rank and station
Are most select and generous in that.
Neither a borrower nor a lender be;
For loan oft loses both itself and friend,   80
And borrowing dulls the edge of husbandry.
This above all: to thine own self be true.

In groups, students translate these lines into modern English. My fifth-period class translated the advice as follows:

✖ Keep your thoughts to yourself. Don't be too quick to act on your thinking.
✖ Be known, but don't step out of bounds. Don't try to be everyone's friend.
✖ Once you find a true friend, hold on tight. They are hard to find.
✖ Don't be quick to start a fight, but once you are in one, fight hard.
✖ Listen to many, but talk to few. Hear the opinion of others, but don't judge people.
✖ Buy expensive, but not tacky, clothes. People will judge you by what you wear. Look nice.
✖ Don't borrow money and don't lend it. If you lend money to a friend, you might lose both.
✖ Be true to yourself. If you are true to yourself, you cannot be false to others.

Even 400 years later, this is one of wisest passages I know. After they complete these translations, I give each group of students one of the bullets of advice and ask them to find an example in the real world where someone did not follow this advice. See Figure 3.2 for some of their real-world examples.

Advice found in Hamlet	Real-world example where the advice wasn't followed
Keep your thoughts to yourself. Don't be too quick to act on your thinking.	Hillary Clinton suggesting that she would stay in the race, citing the fact that Robert Kennedy was assassinated in June. Barack Obama commenting that blue-collar workers cling to guns and religion. President Bush declaring, "Mission accomplished."
Be known, but don't step out of bounds. Don't try to be everyone's friend.	A teenager who accepted over 2,500 friends on her MySpace page ended up being stalked by a molester.
Once you find a true friend, hold on tight. They are hard to find.	The six signs of a "toxic" friend:[a] 1. The Promise Breaker 2. The Double-Crosser 3. The Self-Absorbed 4. The Discloser 5. The Competitor 6. The Fault-Finder
Don't be quick to start a fight, but once you are in one, fight hard.	John Kerry was "swift-boated." He regrets he did not fight back sooner and harder. Obama is responding to criticism immediately.
Listen to many, but talk to few. Hear the opinion of others, but don't judge people.	People did not listen to all sides when some members of the Duke lacrosse team were accused of rape. Public opinion "convicted" the accused before it went to court. It wasn't until months later that the accusations were found to be baseless.
Buy expensive, but not tacky, clothes. People will judge you by what you wear. Look nice.	The following are inappropriate in a job interview and should be avoided:[b] ✖ jeans ✖ anything ripped or stained ✖ shorts ✖ combat pants ✖ trainers ✖ skirts shorter than a few inches above the knee ✖ anything with a large logo or slogan ✖ shoes you can't walk in properly ✖ anything other than shoes that are made of leather or PVC.
Don't borrow money and don't lend it. If you lend money to a friend, you might lose both.	Credit card statistics:[c] ✖ In October 2007, credit card debt that was at least thirty days late totaled $17.6 billion, up 26 percent from October 2006. Some credit card companies, including Advanta, GE Money Bank and HSBC, are reporting a 50 percent increase in accounts that are at least ninety days late compared to the same time last year ✖ In 1968, consumers' total credit debt was $8 billion (in current dollars). In 2008 the total exceeds $880 billion.
Be true to yourself. If you are true to yourself, you cannot be false to others.	Robert DeNiro used to make movies like *The Deer Hunter* and *Raging Bull*. He now makes *Meet the Fockers* and *Bullwinkle*.

FIGURE 3.2

Hamlet QUOTES

[a]Source: *When Friendship Hurts*, by Jan Yager.
[b]Source: Answerbag.com.
[c]Source: www.hoffmanbrinker.com/credit-card-debt-statistics.html.

When students are exposed to the wisdom found in *Hamlet* (or any other major literary work) and recognize what happens to those in today's world who fail to heed that wisdom, they begin to understand that there is real value in reading the play. It's not just a story; it's an imaginative rehearsal for living a productive life as an adult. And this wisdom is not just found in the advice scene, it is packed throughout the play.

Start with the Guided Tour; End with the Budget Tour

My friend Carol Jago recommends that we begin each book with a guided tour. That is, we roll up our sleeves and actively do everything we can to ease students into academic reading. This means that we frame the text before students read it. We provide a specific purpose for reading each chapter. We design close readings that enable kids to delve deeper than surface-level reading. We model to students how we would read the text. In short, we give students a hands-on guided tour of the front half of the book. We craft lessons so that students have ample time to discuss their ideas and their confusion, both in small-group and whole-class settings.

About halfway through the novel, Jago argues, we should shift to budget tour mode. In other words, we should begin to step out of the process and begin requiring our students to take the journey on their own. Once students have enough framing, once they have become familiar with the rhythm and structure of the text, once they have begun to make sense of this unfamiliar world we have immersed them in, then it is time for the teacher to step to the background and allow them to read the text on their own. Teachers should not hold the hands of their students all the way through the novel. If the front half of the book is taught properly (more on this in Chapter 4), students should be equipped to read the second half of the book with much less assistance from the instructor. Students should be encouraged to transition from the guided tour into the budget tour.

Augment Books Instead of Flogging Them

Philosopher Kenneth Burke's (1968) notion is that the real value in reading literature is that it provides our students with imaginative rehearsals for the real world. It is imperative that we augment every novel our students read with real-world text that shows them that the book they are reading offers valuable insight into living productive lives.

When reading *1984*, for example, my students are placed into groups, and each group is given a different article to read. All the articles address a specific theme from the novel. In *1984*, for example, a central theme concerns what happens to a democracy when a government is given too much surveillance power. My students' groups were given the following articles:

✖ "General Background on the Reauthorization of the Patriot Act." An argument that the Patriot Act has been a valuable tool in fighting terrorism. (http://www.npr.org/news/specials/patriotact/patriotactprovisions.html)

✖ "The Patriot Act: Key Controversies." An argument that the Patriot Act has gone too far when it comes to invading the lives of U.S. citizens. (http://www.npr.org/news/specials/patriotact/deal)

✖ "'Big Brother' Cameras on Watch for Criminals." A story about how the city of Tampa has mounted cameras with face recognition abilities throughout the city. (http://www.usatoday.com/tech/news/2001-08-02-big-brother-cameras .htm)

✖ "U.S. Airport Screeners Are Watching What You Read." People who are pulled from security lines for extra screening often have notes taken about them that are stored in a database for years. (http://www.wired.com/ politics/onlinerights/news/2007/09/flight_tracking)

✖ "Are You a Stalker Too?" How Facebook, MySpace, and Google are used to accumulate information about you. (http://www.latimes.com/news/ opinion/la-oe-daum5apr05,0,6075357.column)

✖ "Companies Use Scans to Track Employees." A number of mainstream corporations are using hand scanners to track the movement of their employees. (http://www.msnbc.msn.com/id/23814798/)

✖ "Friends Under the Microscope." The Spokeo website promises to find things about your friends' online lives "that you never knew about, guaranteed." (http://www.newsweek.com/id/96366)

✖ "George Orwell, Big Brother Is Watching Your House." In Orwell's home country, there are more than 4.2 million surveillance cameras, one for every fourteen people in the country. It is estimated that each person is caught on camera an average of 300 times per day. (http://www.thisislondon.co.uk/ news/article-23391081-details/George+Orwell,+Big+Brother+is+watching +your+house/article.do)

Each group is asked to read a specific article and to capture its big idea on one sheet of paper (or overhead transparency). I do not allow them to write more than ten words on the paper. They may draw or use symbols to augment their ten words. When their reading and discussions are completed, I randomly choose one person from each group to share their article's big idea with the class. This jigsaw gives students exposure to eight different articles in one class period. More important, it illustrates that we are not just reading *1984* to find out what happens to the protagonist, Winston Smith. We read it to find out what is happening in our world today. We read it so students can use it as a vehicle to think about their world. As we work through the novel, we may revisit the jigsaw model as a means for closely examining other themes that pose relevance in my students' world. Beyond surveillance, we conduct other jigsaws to examine how news is biased or to take a look at how language is manipulated to influence the populace.

This is not a strategy used solely in teaching *1984*. I want to augment every book my students read with relevant, real-world text. Google enables me to do this.

Create Topic Floods

Another way to augment books instead of flogging them occurs when I create a topic flood for my students to study. As I write this, for example, the California Supreme Court has controversially ruled to legalize same-sex marriage. When this occurred, I used Google to pull a number of writings on the topic from our two local newspapers, the *Orange County Register* (a conservative newspaper) and the *Los Angeles Times* (a liberal newspaper). I created a topic flood—a packet for each student consisting of numerous new stories, editorials, and letters to the editor. I included a wide spectrum of opinion from both sides of the political spectrum.

Through this topic flood, students were immersed in the topic at hand. Using different color highlighters, they color coded the arguments found on both sides of the issue. Once they were well versed in the topic, this led to interesting debate, which in turn led to the writing of persuasive essays.

I have used numerous topic floods over the years—from O. J. Simpson to 9/11 to same-sex marriage—and every time I have used this strategy students have been highly engaged. As an extra bonus, topic floods strengthen students' prior knowledge, which they will need as thinking adults.

✦ ✦ ✦

Each of the previous strategies has proved successful in getting students interested in reading academic text. But what about getting them more interested in reading recreational works as well? Here are suggestions to move kids away from readicide and back toward lifelong reading:

Adopt a 50/50 approach. As mentioned earlier in this book, a disturbing trend is that students are not given the opportunity to develop recreational reading habits; the focus has been on preparing students for exams, and as such, students are overdosing on a steady diet of academic texts. High-interest reading materials have been set aside. Instead, recreational reading needs to be developed. I love strawberries, but if they were the only food I was allowed to eat, I wouldn't like them for long.

Students need to be reintroduced to the notion that we read for enjoyment. To help my students achieve this goal, I have adopted a 50/50 approach in my classroom. To mix up the reading diet of my students, I want half of their reading to be academic, and I want half of their reading to be recreational. By emphasizing recreational reading, I am not underselling the value of academic texts. As I argued earlier in this chapter, reading difficult text is essential and plays an important role in developing young readers (and young citizens). But students who only read academic texts become students who never read recreational texts. That is unconscionable. To prevent this, young readers need a balance of reading between academic and recreational texts. It may sound simple, but this balance has fallen by the wayside in many schools. This reading imbalance needs immediate attention.

The one-pager. Creating a curriculum in which half of the reading is self-selected creates an accountability problem for teachers. If the teacher infuses the recreational reading experience with too much accountability—chapter questions, worksheets, double-entry journals—then the experience ceases to be recreational. However, if students are never held to any accountability, many of them will not start reading. It is a delicate balance.

I am well aware that as an adult I do not need any accountability when I sit down to read a book. Because I find reading enjoyable, no one needs to dangle a quiz over my head to entice me to read. (In fact, dangling quizzes over our students' heads is part of the problem.) What I have found, however, especially with reluctant readers, is that accountability is needed—not too much to get in the way of a pleasurable reading experience but enough to prompt reading to occur. I achieve this delicate balance in my classroom by assigning one-pagers. To receive an A, B, or C grade in my classroom, each student must read one self-selected recreational book per month. Upon completing each book, students are asked to fill out a one-pager, a process that takes no more than twenty minutes (see Figure 3.3). One-pagers are simply one-page reflections of the books they have just read (see Appendixes B and C for blank versions).

One-pagers are jumping-off points for having book conferences with students. They contain just enough accountability to encourage reading but not too much to ruin the reading experience. They hold students accountable without

Name: Zuleima
Period: 2

One-Pager

Title	Rain of Gold
Author	Victor Villaseñor
Date started / date completed	9/4 (date Completed)
Pages read	.559
Rating of book (1-10)	10

Describe a minor character/person in the book who had major importance. Explain.

Carlota, in my eyes, played a very important role in this novel. Throughout the whole novel, I noticed right away that she was very self centered, egotistical and materialistic. It's funny because this touches upon how people that are less fortunate are either very humble, or are very greedy. She seemed to be the latter of the two. I swear, If Lupe was a little less idependant and cared enough about what her sister thought, she never would have married Salvador. Carlota kept finding reasons to hate him. She is the epitome of materialistic. Not alot was said about her, she was always complaining about every situation her family was put in. As Lupe's big sister, Carlota should have a big influence on her. If it wasn't for Carlota, Lupe would have never gone to the dance that night, and she never would have met Salvador.

Author's purpose: to express and reflect through the telling of the story of his family coming to America and making a living for themselves.

Intended audience(s): New generations of Americans who are struggling to fit in a new counsry.

Academic honesty
By signing below I am indicating that the information on this page is accurate:

Zuleima

FIGURE 3.3
ONE-PAGER EXAMPLE

killing them. For examples of other one-pager templates, see Appendix C, where you will find an example for each month of the school year.

Remember the three ingredients to building a reader. Three ingredients are foundational to building young readers:

1. *They must have interesting books to read.* Rather than waiting for students to discover the joys of the library, we must bring the books to the students. Students need to be surrounded by interesting books daily, not just on those occasional days when the teacher takes them to the library.
2. *They must have time to read the books inside of school.* Because many of our students leave school and head straight for soccer practice or to after-school jobs, or because many of students make a beeline to their video game consoles, it is imperative that some time be carved out of each school day for reading.
3. *They must have a place to read their books.* School is the only place where we can control what occurs in our students' lives. If we are serious about developing readers, we have to take advantage of our time together by making school a place where reading occurs.

Jon Scieszka, author of *The Stinky Cheese Man* and other high-interest books for young readers, has recently been named the first U.S. Ambassador for Young People's Literature. Scieszka, a fan of "stupid book" reading, is traveling the country reminding parents and teachers of the importance of finding high-interest reading material for reluctant readers. The way Scieszka (Strauss 2008, B2) sees it, parents and teachers should

✖   give children much more freedom to choose what they want to read rather than what adults think they should read. (This aligns with the 50/50 approach discussed earlier in this chapter.)

✖   expand the definition of reading to more than novels. "Nonfiction, graphic novels, comic books, magazines, online, audiobooks—I think all that works. It all helps turn kids into readers" (Strauss 2008, B2).

✖   stop demonizing other media. "Don't make computers and TV and movies the bad guy. Those things aren't going to go away. I think we did ourselves a disservice in the past by saying TV is bad, reading is good. It's not that cut and dried (Strauss 2008, B2).

Scieszka warns of the reader's death spiral, which goes like this: "It's where kids aren't reading and then are worse at reading because they aren't reading, and then they read less because it is hard and they get worse, and then they see themselves as non-readers" (Strauss 2008, B2). Giving students "stupid" books and other high-interest reading material is the first line of defense against students' falling into the reader's death spiral. Unfortunately, teachers often accelerate the death spiral by insisting that all reading be academic in nature and that each book students read must be sliced and diced a million different ways. The death spiral ends in readicide.

Finding the "Sweet Spot" of Instruction

The road to readicide is paved with the chop-chop reading philosophy widely found in our schools. Overteaching books not only prevents students from achieving reading flow, it creates instruction that values trivial thinking over deeper thinking and damages our students' prospects for becoming lifelong readers. Paradoxically, this chapter is going to address another key contributor to readicide—the underteaching of books. This may seem strange coming on the heels of a chapter that argues that there is too much teaching going on, but simply handing students difficult books and asking them to fend for themselves is not the answer either. There is a huge difference between assigning reading and teaching reading, and students need teachers who recognize the balance between chopping books to death and handing books to students without the proper level of support. I contend that students who are handed *The Grapes of Wrath* to read without any help from the teacher often reach the same level of readicide as those students stuck in a classroom plodding through a 122-page curriculum guide. Underteaching can be as damaging as overteaching, and this chapter will explore what we, as teachers, can do to give our students the proper level of instructional support without abandoning them or without drowning them in a sea of sticky notes, double-entry journals, and worksheets.

Teaching Matters

In examining the area of instruction found between overteaching and under-teaching, we need to examine the overall importance the teacher plays in the classroom. In "Good Teaching Matters: How Well-Qualified Teachers Can Close the Gap," Kati Haycock (1998), director of The Education Trust, notes that the difference between a good teacher and a bad teacher can be a full level of achievement in a single school year. Haycock cites a number of studies:

- A study conducted in Tennessee showed that "on average, the least-effective teachers produced gains of about 14 percentile points during the school year. By contrast, the most-effective teachers posted gains among low-achieving students that averaged 55 percentile points" (1998, 4). The Tennessee data also showed "dramatic differences for middle- and high-achieving students, too. For example, high-achieving students gain an average of only 2 points under the direction of least-effective teachers but an average of 25 points under the guidance of most-effective teachers. Middle achievers gain a mere 10 points with least-effective teachers but realize point gains in the mid-30s with the most-effective teachers" (1998, 5). Haycock highlights the long-term effects of teaching when she notes that "even two years after the fact, the performance of fifth-grade students is still affected by the quality of their third-grade teachers" (1998, 6).
- A study of teacher effectiveness in Dallas of an average group of fourth graders found that those students "assigned to highly effective teachers three years in a row rose from the 59th percentile in fourth grade to the 76th percentile by the conclusion of sixth grade. A fairly similar (but slightly higher achieving) group of students were assigned three consecutive ineffective teachers and fell from the 60th percentile in the fourth grade to the 42nd percentile by the end of the sixth grade" (1998, 7). Haycock reminds us that "a gap of this magnitude—34 percentile points—for students who started off roughly the same is hugely significant" (1998, 7).
- A study in Boston demonstrated that although "the gains of students with the top-third teachers were slightly below the national median for growth (5.6 compared to 8.0 nationally), the students with teachers from the bottom third showed virtually no growth" (1998, 9-10). When the numbers are examined further, they show "that one third of Boston public school teachers are producing six times the learning seen in the bottom third" (1998, 10).

These studies strongly demonstrate the importance teaching plays in student achievement. Having a good teacher versus having a poor teacher, particularly in the early years, can determine whether a young student is put in an honors track or a remedial track. As Haycock notes, a student's teacher may determine the difference "between entry to a selective college and a lifetime at a burger joint" (1998, 10).

Haycock's findings are echoed in a study conducted by the National Institute of Child Health and Human Development Early Child Care Research Network (Pianta et al. 2007). Researchers spent thousands of hours in more than 2,500 first-, third-, and fifth-grade classrooms tracking students through elementary school. Among their findings:

✖ The typical child "stands only a one-in-fourteen chance of having a consistently rich, supportive elementary school experience" (1).

✖ Teachers are spending way too much time on drill-and-kill activities. As a result, students are not getting enough time developing deeper problem-solving and reasoning skills.

✖ Students are spending way too much time listening to their teachers and not enough time developing critical thinking skills through collaborative work.

✖ An overemphasis on basic reading and writing skills comes at a significant cost; students are getting less instruction in science and social science. Their prior knowledge and background experiences, those experiences foundational to becoming strong readers, are being narrowed.

✖ The typical teacher scored only 3.6 out of 7 points for "richness of instructional methods" and 3.4 for providing "evaluative feedback" to students on their work (1).

✖ Students in private schools did not fare any better than students in public schools.

The lead researcher, Robert Pianta of the University of Virginia, notes that his findings support previous research that has found that highly skilled, engaging teachers can help close the achievement gap. Unfortunately, only one out of every fourteen kids are in a consistent classroom environment that helps them do so. The study found little difference between experienced teachers and inexperienced teachers or between those teachers deemed "highly qualified" and those deemed average. What does this mean? Unfortunately, it suggests there are a lot of experienced and "highly qualified" teachers out there drilling and killing. They are playing a significant role in maintaining the achievement gap, and, when the achievement gap is maintained, readicide occurs.

Finding the Sweet Spot

To understand where the most effective teaching occurs, it might help to introduce a term used in baseball and other sports—the "sweet spot." In baseball, the
sweet spot is the spot on the bat that, when hit, carries the ball the farthest.
Unfortunately, batters don't always hit the sweet spot. Sometimes they are
jammed and hit the ball off the handle; other times they swing too soon and hit
the ball off the end of the bat (which can really hurt the hands). When the sweet
spot is missed, the result is almost always the same: the batter is out. However,
when the ball hits the sweet spot, the batter knows it immediately. The ball really
flies. Hitters describe the feeling of hitting the sweet spot as "true" or "pure."

When motivating adolescents to read, I am constantly searching for the
sweet spot of instruction. Teaching matters, but what kind of teaching matters
most? Where is the reading sweet spot? It certainly is not found buried in a 122-
page curriculum guide. However, it is also not found when we hand students
books that are too difficult for them and ask them to navigate on their own. The
sweet spot lies somewhere between these two extreme instructional approaches.

In exploring where that sweet spot might be, it is wise to start with what we
know works, and when I start with what I know works, I always return to the
work of Nancie Atwell. I can't think of a single professional book that has shaped
my thinking about the teaching of reading more than *In the Middle* (Atwell
1998), which remains the eminent call for teachers to "come out from behind
their desks to write with, listen to, and learn" from young readers and writers
(Atwell 1998, 12). She reminds us that we, the teachers, are the best readers and
writers in our classroom, and as such, each of us should be a "mentor," a "medi-
ator," and a "model" (21). Atwell's model for setting up a reader's workshop—
surrounding students with tons of high-interest reading materials, providing
students with ample reading choice, carving out significant time in the school
day to read, conducting reading mini-lessons to help students find the reading
zone—is still a model I emulate and one that I recommend to new and experienced teachers alike. Certainly, developing our students' recreational reading
habits play a crucial part in helping them to discover the reading flow. We all
have been so lost in a book that we lose track of time and place, and we want our
students to discover this experience. In this quest, Atwell's work has been indis-
pensable in building the recreational reading habits of my students.

However, when it comes to helping students become excellent readers of difficult texts, finding the sweet spot of teaching becomes more problematic. It is
much easier for a student to find reading flow while reading *Harry Potter* than it
is for them to find reading flow while reading *Hamlet*. This is where the impor-

tance of teaching comes into play. If we overteach *Hamlet*, we not only run the risk of killing the play, we also run the risk of creating a dislike of reading that may spill over into recreational and academic reading. However, if we under-teach *Hamlet*, students will drown (or turn to CliffsNotes for rescue). Both of these approaches produce dead readers.

Works such as *Hamlet*, *1984*, and *The Grapes of Wrath* are why you and I are in the classroom. Most students cannot navigate these works expertly on their own. Our expertise is needed, and how this expertise is applied will determine whether our students have meaningful reading experiences. So how can we approach difficult works such as *Hamlet* in our classrooms in a way that will not kill off our reluctant readers? Certainly, as Chapter 3 illustrates, chopping up the work into a million pieces is not the answer. Unfortunately, having students fly solo is not the answer either.

"Lousy Classic" Is an Oxymoron

In *The Reading Zone*, Atwell (2007) reminds us that high school students "are trying to make sense of adulthood—it is really just around the corner now—but their schools too often engage them in a version of reading that is so limiting and so demanding, so bereft of intentionality or personal meaning, that what they learn is to forgo pleasure reading and its satisfactions and, for four years, 'do English'" (107). In moving away from doing English, Atwell suggests that students "learn how to select: Which books do they need to let settle inside themselves? Which are page-turners, about which there isn't a whole lot to say? And which do they want to think about more deeply and consider as works of art by writing about them?" (2007, 115).

As much as I respect Atwell, this is where she and I part. For one thing, in my school district, and in most of the districts that I have visited across the country, particular titles are mandated in the curriculum. Nearly every ninth-grade student in the United States reads *Romeo and Juliet*. Other classics, such as *To Kill a Mockingbird*, *The Great Gatsby*, and *Julius Caesar*, are taught nationwide because they are required. Most teachers don't have the wiggle room in their school year to deviate from the required readings. These are the books they have on their shelves, and their school boards and district offices have dictated they be taught.

I also differ from Atwell because I believe a required reading canon is a good thing and that there is a real value that can only be found when the entire class is reading the same title. When every student in the country reads *Romeo and Juliet*, it means we all acquire a shared cultural literacy, a sharing that is foundational if we, as a culture, are going to be able to communicate with one another (for more on this, see Hirsch's *The Knowledge Deficit* [2006]). Beyond gaining cultural literacy, students who read assigned classics will receive adequate practice when it comes to reading demanding texts. Thus, rigor is not avoided; it is guaranteed. Furthermore, wrestling with *Romeo and Juliet* in a whole-class setting produces richer conversation and deeper thinking than occurs when the work is read individually or in small groups.

As much as I understand how doing English has ruined books for students such as Mem Fox's daughter, Chloe, all students should be required to do English, meaning all students should be required to wrestle with "limiting" and "demanding" works. All students should be engaged in books they might normally avoid. This doesn't mean it has to be an awful, reader-killing experience. If taught in the sweet spot, *Hamlet* should be a work that motivates students to take additional English classes, not convince them to avoid English courses at all costs. *Hamlet* isn't the problem; the problem lies in how the work is taught (or how the work is not taught). Doing English is not the issue; how students do English is the issue. The question isn't whether classics should be taught; the question is how do we get students reading classics to reach the sweet spot?

Identifying the Sweet Spot

When I bring a difficult book into the classroom for students to read, I always struggle with my level of involvement. How much help is too much help? How much help is too little help? What is the right balance? Let's address this delicate balance by first examining the experiences of my daughter, Devin, who was asked to read two difficult books in her high school English class. First, she was given *The Grapes of Wrath* to read on her own. She was not given any purpose or focus. The book was not "framed" at all. Like a good student, she struggled through most of the text, finally giving up from "sheer boredom." She admits now that she turned to SparkNotes to get her to the finish line. When the due date came, she was given a test and an essay question. Now, two years later, she tells me the book "is horrible," and she does "not remember a single thing in it." And she's a good reader.

Later that year her class read *The Adventures of Huckleberry Finn*. They were asked to stop repeatedly to work with the text. They had to choose scenes they thought exhibited different levels of satire and go home and film these scenes from the book. They spent hours filming, editing, and presenting these scenes. Not surprisingly, after all this chop-chop, Devin finds *Huckleberry Finn* "stupid and pointless."

Devin graduated from high school in 2008 still believing that *The Grapes of Wrath* and *The Adventures of Huckleberry Finn* are awful books. She is wrong, of course; they both hold great value to the modern reader, but this is how readicide occurs when books are undertaught (*The Grapes of Wrath*) or overtaught (*The Adventures of Huckleberry Finn*). If a student reads a major literary work, and exits the work finding it "bereft of intentionality or personal meaning" (Atwell 2007, 107), this is an indictment of the teaching of that work, not of the work itself. Classics found in the canon are there for a reason; there is a wisdom, a universality of truth found in them that helps the modern reader to garner a deeper comprehension of today's world. I am a wiser adult because I have read *The Grapes of Wrath*, even though it was written in 1939. Because our students are at an age in which they are trying to make sense of adulthood, they need exposure to as many other wise works as possible. These books provide our students imaginative rehearsals for the real world, and in today's complex world, our students need as many of these rehearsals as possible.

So it is here I propose a radical stance: there is no such thing as a lousy classic. "Lousy classic" is an oxymoron. By its definition, a classic has something valuable in it or it would not have survived as a classic. Those classics you and I hated in high school actually contain greatness. Every one of them. If we were unable to discover this greatness, if we didn't recognize the value found in these books, it's because our teachers did not help us recognize this value. Because a teacher kills a great book by mishandling it doesn't mean the book is stupid and pointless. It means the reader was not put in a position to discover the book's greatness.

In trying to help my students find that greatness, my teaching of classic literature focuses on the value they will take from the works. I am not suggesting that every classic should be liked; in fact, I never focus on whether my students will like the books. Sure, I'd like my students to enjoy the books as much as I do, but it is important that they take away something valuable after wrestling with them. As I said in Chapter 2, I know some of my students will like *1984*, and I know some of my students will not like *1984*, but my goal is that all of them will attain something valuable from their reading. After reading *1984*, for example, I want them to begin to see privacy issues differently. I want them to recognize how language is manipulated. I want them to learn to question authority. These are valuable considerations to take into adulthood. My students might not like *1984*—not all students are enamored of dark, dystopian science fiction—but they will leave this book as wiser, more culturally literate human beings. That concerns me much more than worrying about whether the book is liked.

I am a wiser, more culturally literate human being because I was required to read difficult "texts" in my life. I enjoy museum visits today, for example, because I was required to visit museums with my parents when I was a child. Though I certainly did not start out liking museums—I'd have rather done almost anything than spend a day inside a museum when I was an adolescent. I enjoy the music of Joan Armatrading, even though the first time I listened to her I was put off by her unconventionality. I stuck with it because of a friend's prodding and have since grown to love her music. I enjoy poetry today because I was required to take a course in it in college and was fortunate enough to find a professor who led me to discover its value. Many of the pleasures I enjoy today are a result of the required guidance of others who helped me discover the beauty and value of these pursuits I would not have found had I been left on my own.

Let's never forget there is beauty and value found in reading difficult literature. Our job is to lead our reluctant students to discover this beauty and value.

One of things I like about Atwell's approach is that she eschews the chop-chop philosophy by trusting her students to tackle large chunks of text. As she states, "it just makes sense for English teachers to pass out the books, give students a set amount of time to read them on their own, give a just-the-facts quiz on the day of the deadline if they don't feel the kids can be trusted to read a book without it, then engage in discussions about the whole work of art that the author intended and created, just as many of these students will in their college English classes" (Atwell 2007, 115).

Atwell, of course, is illuminating the dangers that occur when we do not trust our students to read long passages of text. When a good book gets chopped up too much, it ceases to be a good book. However, I cannot hand my students challenging literary works and tell them I will meet them at the finish line. They simply do not have the skills to take that journey on their own. I am a teacher, not an assigner, and my students need me most while they are reading. My job is twofold: (1) to introduce my students to books that are a shade too hard for them and (2) to use my expertise to help them navigate these texts in a way that brings value to their reading experience. Let's explore what achieving these two goals might look like in a classroom.

What You Can Do to Prevent Readicide

The following are specific suggestions on how to find the sweet spot when teaching difficult literature to adolescents.

Recognize the Importance of Framing

Let's revisit the importance that framing a text plays in reading comprehension. Read the following passage and score your level of comprehension on a scale of 1 to 10:

> The pitcher's stuff was filthy. He was bringing cheese. He mixed in some chin music. Along with the heat, Uncle Charlie would occasionally show his face, producing a number of bowel-lockers. Only two batters got a knock. No one came close to dialing 8.

How well did you score? The answer to that question hinges more on your knowledge of baseball than it does on your reading ability. People who know baseball will comprehend the passage completely. People who are unfamiliar with baseball will say it looks like gibberish. You might be an excellent reader, but if your baseball knowledge is limited, you will need considerable assistance to reach even the simplest level of comprehension. (For the uninitiated in baseball, Figure 4.1 provides a translation.)

What does this mean for teachers when we teach difficult books? That what we do before students begin reading is paramount. For many of my reluctant

Original Text	Translation
The pitcher's stuff was filthy.	The pitcher had excellent control, and his pitches were very difficult to hit.
He was bringing cheese.	He was throwing the ball exceptionally hard.
He mixed in some chin music.	To keep batters from crowding the plate, the pitcher mixed in some high and tight pitches.
Along with the heat, Uncle Charlie would occasionally show his face, producing a number of bowel-lockers.	Along with his fastball, the pitcher occasionally threw curveballs. Some of them were so effective they froze the batters in their tracks.
Only two batters got a knock.	Only two batters got a hit.
No one came close to dialing 8.	No one came close to hitting a home run (8 is the first number used in most hotel rooms to dial long distance).

FIGURE 4.1
BASEBALL CHART

readers, the difficult texts that I am requiring them to read look like gibberish as well. For example, let's take one of the difficult texts that I require my students to read, Robert Louis Stevenson's classic mystery, *The Strange Case of Dr. Jekyll and Mr. Hyde*. Looking at the first paragraph of the novel reinforces the notion that this is not a book I can simply hand my reluctant students to read:

> *Mr. Utterson the lawyer was a man of a rugged countenance that was never lighted by a smile; cold, scanty and embarrassed in discourse; backward in sentiment; lean, long, dusty, dreary and yet somehow lovable. At friendly meetings, and when the wine was to his taste, something eminently human beaconed from his eye; something indeed which never found its way into his talk, but which spoke not only in these silent symbols of the after-dinner face, but more often and loudly in the acts of his life. He was austere with himself; drank gin when he was alone, to mortify a taste for vintages; and though he enjoyed the theater, had not crossed the doors of one for twenty years. But he had an approved tolerance for others; sometimes wondering, almost with envy, at the high pressure of spirits involved in their misdeeds; and in any extremity inclined to help rather than to reprove. "I incline to Cain's heresy," he used to say quaintly: "I let my brother go to the devil in his own way." In this character, it was frequently his fortune to be the last reputable acquaintance and the last good influence in the lives of downgoing men. And to such as these, so long as they came about his chambers, he never marked a shade of change in his demeanour.* (Stevenson 1886, 1)

From experience, I know that I cannot simply assign Chapter 1 of *Dr. Jekyll and Mr. Hyde* to my students and ask them to get started. I have to prepare them for the reading by "framing" the text. This framing might include:

✖ A preview of the final exam essay question so as to provide a very specific reading purpose for the novel.
✖ Some vocabulary preview to help them with the archaic language.
✖ A discussion of the historical context of the story. An explanation of how the time in which it was written (the Victorian Age) contributes to the meaning of the work.
✖ Background on the author and what he was trying to accomplish with this work.
✖ An anticipation guide to help students begin recognizing the universal truths found in the novel.
✖ A discussion on why we are reading this book and the value it offers to the modern reader.

These steps are taken *before* the reading of the novel commences. Remember, this kind of framing is not necessary when students are reading recreationally. My students do not need a teacher's expertise to begin reading a Harry Potter or Gossip Girl book. But reading *Dr. Jekyll and Mr. Hyde*, and other books of equal difficulty, is a different matter. By the nature of their difficulty, they require a teacher's presence, and if readicide is to be avoided, this presence should be asserted before students encounter page one.

Remember the Value Found in Second-Draft (and Third-Draft) Reading

I have taught *Romeo and Juliet* for more than twenty years now and I have never had a student stop me in the middle of act 1, scene 1, and ask excitedly, "Mr. Gallagher, do you notice what theme is developing here?" On the contrary, they ask questions that typically come from teenage readers struggling through a first-draft reading:

"What is happening?"
"Who is a Capulet?"
"Who is a Montague?"
"What side is Romeo on?"
"What side is Juliet on?"
And my favorite: "Who the heck would name their kid 'Benvolio'?"

Students in this stage of reading are in survival mode, simply struggling to understand the text on a literal level. If I have framed the text properly, I will have helped them to achieve this initial level of comprehension (a level that is foundational before deeper reading can occur). But there is a much richer level of craft inside most classic works of literature—a level of beauty that usually is not discovered until students revisit the text on a second-draft (or third-draft) reading. I might add that most students will only discover the deeper, richer level of comprehension found in a second-draft reading through the guidance of a teacher. To illustrate this idea, let's revisit the first paragraph of *Dr. Jekyll and Mr. Hyde*, but this time, you will read it with a specific purpose in mind. As you reread it, look for the opposites that Stevenson has intentionally embedded in the text. In this first paragraph, there are at least nine of them, beginning with one in the first sentence:

Mr. Utterson the lawyer was a man of a rugged countenance that was never lighted by a smile; cold, scanty and embarrassed in discourse; backward in sentiment; lean, long, dusty, dreary and yet somehow lovable. At friendly meetings, and when the wine was to his taste, something eminently human beaconed from his eye; something indeed which never found its way into his talk, but which spoke not only in these silent symbols of the after-dinner face, but more often and loudly in the acts of his life. He was austere with himself; drank gin when he was alone, to mortify a taste for vintages; and though he enjoyed the theater, had not crossed the doors of one for twenty years. But he had an approved tolerance for others; sometimes wondering, almost with envy, at the high pressure of spirits involved in their misdeeds; and in any extremity inclined to help rather than to reprove. "I incline to Cain's heresy," he used to say quaintly: "I let my brother go to the devil in his own way." In this character, it was frequently his fortune to be the last reputable acquaintance and the last good influence in the lives of downgoing men. And to such as these, so long as they came about his chambers, he never marked a shade of change in his demeanour.

How many did you find?

Opposites Found in the First Paragraph of Robert Louis Stevenson's *Dr. Jekyll and Mr. Hyde*

Mr. Utterson was cold, dreary.	Mr. Utterson was lovable.
He was a lawyer.	He didn't like to talk.
He spoke quietly.	His actions spoke loudly.
He had something "eminently human beacon from his eye."	This humaneness never found it into his speech.
He enjoyed the theater.	He never went to the theater.
A reference is made to the Bible.	A reference is made to the Devil.
He was a good influence . . .	. . . on downgoing men.
He liked to help.	He did not like to reprove.
He was an upright (and uptight) citizen.	He sometimes looked at his defendants "with envy."

I have taught this novel for many years, and I have shared it with many teacher groups, and not once while reading the first paragraph has a reader ever raised a hand and said, "Do you notice that Stevenson has hidden many opposites in his writing?" Because readers are in "survival mode" when they read this chapter for the first time, discovery of the opposites embedded in the text is something that only happens on a rereading of the text, and this is a discovery that only happens when the teacher provides that specific purpose for revisiting the text.

You might ask, "Why have them revisit the text to look for opposites? What value is there in that?" I have my students read the text in search of opposites because even as they begin to read the novel I have the final exam question in mind:

> Discuss Stevenson's idea of duality in *Dr. Jekyll and Mr. Hyde* and share how this duality is still found in today's world.

On the final exam, students are then asked to pick a topic in today's world and discuss its duality. Last year, their essays ranged from looking at both sides of humankind's treatment of the environment, to particular political candidates who have flip-flopped, to both the wonders and the abuses of the Catholic Church. This is the real value that emanates from reading *Dr. Jekyll and Mr. Hyde*—when my students are able to recognize Stevenson's duality in their world. *Dr. Jekyll and Mr. Hyde* prepares my students to understand that everything has two sides, and when they are able to recognize this they become much better equipped to read politicians, to read advertisements, to read ballot initiatives. Again, they might end up liking *Dr. Jekyll and Mr. Hyde,* or they might end up not liking it, but after they've finished reading it, my students will have mined some value from reading the novel and will be better equipped to read and negotiate today's world. This new, sharper lens is rarely, if ever, developed without the guidance of a teacher.

Adopt a "Big Chunk/Little Chunk" Philosophy

If students aren't directed to read small chunks of text closely, they will never learn to reach deeper levels of analysis. However, if we chop up the books and have them analyze too many segments, they will succumb to readicide. It is a delicate balance, one that I try to achieve with what I call a "big chunk/little chunk approach." In the simplest terms, students do a lot of first-draft reading of large chunks of text on their own (after initial framing from the teacher). This is followed with second- and third-draft close readings of excerpts in the classroom (which require teacher expertise). In the *Dr. Jekyll and Mr. Hyde* example, the search for opposites occurs after students complete a first-draft reading of Chapter 1. Once they return to class, I redirect their attention to a feature of the novel (in this case the opposites) they would most likely not have discovered on their own.

Students must be eased into large chunk reading. Once the work is properly framed and my students are ready to commence reading, I often read the first few pages aloud to them, often pausing to think out loud. I am the best reader in the room, and as such, it is imperative that I let them in on how I tackle the initial confusion of a new book. I want my students to know that reading difficult text is hard even for the teacher—that it is normal to be confused. I wrestle with the text in front of them, and in doing so, will often have students chart the strategies I use to make sense of the book. By modeling my own confusion, and by demonstrating how I cope with the confusion, my students are eased into the difficult text.

At some point early on, however, my students are pushed to accept the challenge of reading large chunks of the book on their own. I am aiming for flow that only occurs when readers are stretched. Achieving flow in recreational books is one thing; finding flow in academic text, however, is much more difficult. To help students find this flow, I almost always provide a purpose for their reading before they read the assigned large chunk. Because reading a new novel or work of nonfiction can be overwhelming, I ask my students to focus on only one or two elements while they read. I provide a specific purpose for the reading that scaffolds students toward the final exam essay.

Take Barbara Kingsolver's *The Bean Trees,* for example. Before my students read it, I hand them the final exam question:

Discuss Kingsolver's central theme and how this theme emerges through the author's use of symbolism.

Before my students begin reading, they already know what lens they are going to read this book through (examining the symbolism found in the novel). After framing the text by explaining its historical context and by previewing some vocabulary, I begin reading the novel with them, pausing to model my thinking out loud. Once they are eased into the book, I start assigning large chunks of reading. For example, I might frame the first chapter with the following instructions: "Please take Chapter 1 home and finish reading it tonight. Remember, you are reading this chapter with the idea of looking for possible symbolism in the novel. With this in mind, you will note in tonight's chapter that the author makes references to things that grow. Pay attention to this. If you do so, I think you may have some insight by the end of this chapter as to why Kingsolver titled her novel *The Bean Trees.* I would like each of you to come to class tomorrow with a brief reflection in your writer's notebook on what all these references to things that grow might mean." My students then begin reading the large chunk of text with this specific purpose in mind.

When students return to class the next day, they share their thinking. To make sure they are focusing in the direction I have chosen, we shift to a close reading (which, in actuality, is a rereading). To facilitate this, I have prepared a focused reading for them—a small chunk from last night's chapter that they will reread closely to hone their analytical skills. I am not chopping up the entire chapter; rather, we are revisiting one small piece taken from a large chapter they have already read.

To prepare my students for a close reading, I share Patricia Kain's "How to Do a Close Reading" (1998), which was developed at the Writing Center at Harvard University. Kain introduces students to the three important steps of conducting a close reading:

1. **Read with a pencil in hand, and annotate the text.** This entails "underlining or highlighting key words and phrases—anything that strikes you as surprising or significant, or that raises questions—as well as making notes in the margins" (1).
2. **Look for patterns in the things you've noticed about the text—repetitions, contradictions, similarities.** In the case of *The Bean Trees*, my students look for those patterns that might hint at the author's use of symbolism.
3. **Ask questions about the patterns you've noticed—especially "how" and "why."** Why, for example, does the notion of planting things and nourishing them recur throughout the novel?

In Figure 4.2, you will see an example of a ninth-grade student's close read. Alex had read a large chunk of text the night before, and when he returned to class, he was asked to reread this specific passage. This close read was chosen with the final exam question in mind. Notice Alex is moving in the direction of the prompt when he states, "Hmm . . . I smell a metaphor." Close reads are invaluable in getting students to deeper levels of comprehension. Without them, many students will not move beyond surface-level comprehension.

The big chunk/little chunk approach to reading academic texts addresses both worlds. By assigning large chunks of reading, students can get into a reading flow; at the same time, through occasional carefully selected close readings, students have a chance to sharpen their analytical skills. Once the students hit stride with the book, I lengthen the chunks they read. It might be equally important to recognize what this approach doesn't do: it doesn't chop the book up into

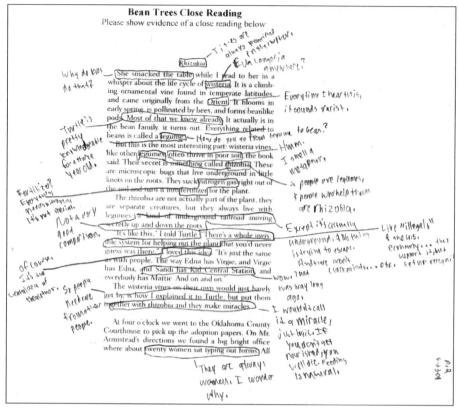

FIGURE 4.2
A CLOSE READING OF *The Bean Trees*

a million pieces, it doesn't value the trivial over the meaningful, and it doesn't try to teach all things in all books. To paraphrase Billy Collins (1996), it doesn't flog the novel with a hose.

Finding the Metacognitive Sweet Spot

According to the Alliance for Excellent Education (2007), many reading researchers once believed "that if students could master the basics of literacy in the first few years of school, that would be sufficient to carry them successfully through the middle and high school years. Increasingly, though, research has made it clear that students need ongoing support in order to handle the more difficult kinds of reading and writing they must do in the upper grades" (1–2). The ongoing support that students need, of course, must come from very active teaching.

To underscore the importance of active teaching, consider this question: have you ever given your students a passage and asked them to highlight what is important? When I ask my students to do this, the results are usually disastrous. They don't discriminately highlight; they color everything! Yet, when I give a passage to adults and ask them to highlight what is important, they do not bathe their passages in highlighter. Unlike students, they are very discriminating when they mark text. Why? Why are mature readers more restrained when identifying what is important? What do mature readers know that immature readers do not know? In this particular example, for instance, adult readers might know where to look to find "what is important." They pay more attention to text structure. They recognize both the author's purpose and intended audience. They have a better idea of where to look in the text, paying closer attention to topic sentences, or knowing where they might find a thesis statement. A mature reader might scan quickly, looking for bold headings, or might skip the body of the passage and go straight to the concluding remarks. In short, mature readers have much better clues than immature readers on how to mark text. We know stuff our students do not know:

What Good and Struggling Readers Do

	Good Readers	Struggling Readers
Before	✖ Think about what they already know / search their prior knowledge	✖ Read without thinking about what they already know
	✖ Identify a purpose for reading the text	✖ Don't know why they are reading text
	✖ Make predictions	✖ Make no predictions
	✖ Have a sense of how major ideas may fit together	✖ Don't have an idea how the major ideas might fit together
During	✖ Pay attention to meaning / are able to identify key information	✖ Overattend to individual words / are often unable to make meaning
	✖ Monitor comprehension while reading	✖ Do not monitor comprehension while reading
	✖ Stop and use "fix-up" strategies	✖ Are unaware of "fix-up" strategies
	✖ Visualize while reading	✖ Are unable to visualize while reading
	✖ Make inferences	✖ Cannot make inferences
	✖ Make connections, both inside and outside the text	✖ Are unable to make connections, both inside and outside the text
	✖ Have a high tolerance for ambiguity	✖ Have a low tolerance for ambiguity
	✖ Ask questions of the text	✖ Do not ask questions of the text
	✖ Are active and engaged	✖ Are passive and unengaged
After	✖ Can summarize	✖ Are often unable to determine main idea(s)
	✖ Understand how ideas fit together	✖ Focus on unimportant or peripheral details
	✖ Can answer implicit, explicit, and application questions	✖ Are unable to answer comprehension questions at various levels
	✖ Can revisit text and make deeper meaning	✖ Are unable to revisit text to make deeper meaning

Adapted from Ciborowski (1992).

In *Deeper Reading* (Gallagher 2004), I discuss *assumicide*, the death of reading that occurs when it is assumed students possess the tools necessary to reach deeper levels of reading. Even as our readers get older, they still need ongoing support to become proficient readers of academic text. From the "What Good and Struggling Readers Do" chart, for example, we know that good readers monitor their comprehension and apply fix-it strategies when their comprehension falters. In short, good readers are consciously strategic when confronted with challenging text.

Unfortunately, many of our students are not strategic when confronted with difficult text. For example, all teachers have participated in the following exchange with a student:

Student: I read the chapter last night but I don't get it.
Teacher: Really? What part did you not get?
Student: All of it.

When a student says, "All of it," what she is really saying is that she doesn't know how to monitor her comprehension. When she gets confused, she simply continues to plow through the text. Good readers, however, do not do this. We have all experienced that feeling of getting to the end of a page and asking ourselves, "What the heck did I just read?" What do we do when this occurs? We stop, gather our focus, back up, and reread. This is not, however, what many of my students do. When they get confused, they keep on reading, thus minimizing their chances of reaching deeper levels of comprehension.

What these examples illustrate, of course, is that in our classrooms we know things about reading that our students do not know. When reading gets tough for us, we consciously choose tools to help us make sense of the text. For example, I had a group of adult readers tackle a difficult passage, and as they read it, they noted the strategies they employed when the reading got hard. Here is what they did:

Reread
Changed speeds
✖   Slowed down when difficulty increased
✖   Skimmed when the reading got easy
Asked about the author
Asked when it was written
Considered how this time frame influenced the author
"Chunked" the text

Read around nonessential clauses
Skipped ahead
Skipped hard parts and returned to them later
Considered the author's purpose
Searched prior knowledge
Highlighted confusion
Considered the author's intended audience
Subvocalized
Visualized
Made predictions
Examined the text structure
Stopped and thought about the passage
Asked questions
Used context to clear confusion
Noticed how the punctuation was used
Paid close attention to the syntax
Made note of italics
Made note of headings
Shifted body position in chair
Told self to focus
Tracked with finger
Paraphrased
Summarized
Commented
Argued with the author
Evaluated the author's idea(s)
Attacked unfamiliar words by looking at the context
Attacked unfamiliar words by looking at prefixes, suffixes, and roots
Lived with ambiguity
Drew conclusions
Made connections to:
✖ Other books
✖ Other films
✖ Other languages
✖ Real-world events
✖ Personal experience

When the reading got hard, good readers used all of the strategies found in this list.
Now, ask yourself the following: when the reading gets hard for your students, how

many of these strategies do they employ? In my classroom, some of my students do some of these strategies, but, unfortunately, some of my students do not know any of these strategies. Many remain at a complete loss when the reading gets hard. Because students don't know what to do when confronted with confusion, these strategies need to be made visible to them, and that is where the teacher is useful.

In determining how and when to make these strategies visible to our students, we must again carefully consider the sweet spot—that area found between underteaching and overteaching. To help us find this sweet spot, it is helpful to define what "underteaching" and "overteaching" of these reading strategies might look like:

Classroom That Underteaches Reading Strategies	Classroom That Overteaches Reading Strategies
✖ Students are given little or no help in understanding what good readers do when the reading gets hard.	✖ Metacognition is overemphasized. Too much time is spent on "noticing what you notice" as a reader.
✖ Discussion is always based on what the text says; little attention is paid to how understanding is reached.	✖ The text gets lost in overanalyzing what is done to make sense of the text.

Teaching Both the Reading and the Reader

In *The Reading Zone*, Atwell (2007) implores teachers, "Do not risk ruining the reading of stories by teaching children to focus on how they're processing them" (63). Atwell asks "teachers to consider whether a curriculum of study skills is the soundest way to help students become skilled, passionate, habitual, critical readers of the stories we—and they—adore" (63). It's an important point. If you want to kill the love of reading in a student, plant innumerable stop signs in the text that will require the student to examine his reading processes at each stop.

Atwell's advice is particularly true when it comes to reading recreational books. Right now I am reading Robert Crais's *The Watchman*, a lightweight but highly entertaining crime novel. However, if you stood over my shoulder and repeatedly asked me how I was making meaning from this text, it would not take long for me to hate this book. I don't need to root around in my metacognitive toolbox to make sense of this book. I am already in the flow. Leave me alone.

Reading much more difficult text, however, poses a different problem. Although I appreciate Atwell's warning that we risk ruining books when we ask students to look at how they are processing them, I have found my students can't process them until they become explicitly aware of those things good readers do. The texts are so hard that they have to look at how they are processing them, or the processing itself will not occur. These are not books that we can curl up at the beach with and fall into an immediate reading flow. These are books that require the teacher to be in the room, and as such, they require a different approach.

As a teacher, I know what good readers do when reading difficult text (as evidenced by the previous list). Ignoring or withholding this information from students might be a good idea when they are reading a Lemony Snicket book, but it is a recipe for readicide when they are reading *Dr. Jekyll and Mr. Hyde*. When tackling difficult text, underteaching can be as damaging as overteaching. Atwell (2007), for example, cites Julie Lausé, a high school English teacher in New Orleans, who was worried that meaningful reading experiences were getting lost because teachers were overteaching the books. To avoid the chop-chop approach, "Lausé distributed all the school's required readings at once, in September—in tenth grade honors English, that was eight books—then assigned deadlines across the school year for the completion of each title, based on what she had determined as the speed of the slowest reader in the class. She and her students discussed each assigned book following its deadline, as a whole work, not in a chapter-by-chapter analysis, and she noted the 'increased depth' of those literary conversations" (Atwell 2007, 111).

I admire how Lausé avoids the chop-chop approach by handing students books and giving them deadlines to read all the works, but I can say unequivocally that this approach would not work with my students. Unlike Lausé, I do not teach honors-level classes, which means I am working with students who come to each book with far less reading experience and thus far less prior knowledge. I cannot simply hand students who are unaware of the Holocaust copies of Elie Wiesel's *Night* and ask them to have it read by October 15. I cannot hand a ninth-grader who is reading at the sixth-grade level a copy of *Romeo and Juliet* and ask him to have it read by Thanksgiving. My students are ill-equipped to take these reading journeys on their own. These books are rigorous and heavy. Without their teacher involved, my students will either give up or make a beeline to CliffsNotes. These works must be taught, and they must be taught while the books are being read.

The challenge, of course, is not overdoing it. So what is the proper balance between underteaching and overteaching those metacognitive skills that good readers employ? To explore this question, let me share an anecdote from one of my freshman classes. They were reading *Night*, and I had framed Chapter 1 for them, eased them into the first few pages, given them a purpose for that night's reading, and asked them to go home and read Chapter 1. When they came back the next day, I had prepared a close reading—a revisitation of a chunk of text. As they worked on their close reading, I gave them highlighters and had them monitor their comprehension by marking spots they found confusing. I circled the room, taking note where they were confused.

The close reading led to a rich discussion, and soon I glanced at the clock and noticed there were four minutes left in the period. My students keep a chart in their notebooks titled, "What Good Readers Do." I had them take them out.

"I noticed as I walked around the room," I said, "that many of you have highlighted the word 'genocide' as a word you do not know. Mike, I noticed that you did not mark the word. Does that mean you know what it means?"

"I am not entirely sure," Mike replied, "but I think it has something to do with death."

"What makes you think that?" I asked.

"Well, it ends with 'cide'," he said. "It reminds me of suicide, homicide. So I think it has something to do with death."

"And pesticide," someone in the back of the class added.

"Good job," I replied. "Mike has done something that good readers do. (Turning to class.) What did Mike do when he didn't understand the word 'genocide'?"

"He looked at the parts of the word," someone replied.

"Right," I said. "Good readers attack unfamiliar words. Take out your 'What Good Readers Do Chart' and add 'attack the word' to it" (as students do this, I also write "attack the word" on a master list of "What Good Readers Do" on the overhead projector). I look up at the clock and notice there are still two minutes remaining in the period. I have a brief discussion with the students about where a word might be attacked—prefix, root, suffix—and then I give them a word to practice before the bell rings.

"Quickly," I add. "Try attacking a different word." I write the word "unenviable" on the board, and they spend the last minute of class attacking the word. We share some thinking on the word and the last thing they hear me say before they leave is, "Remember this as readers when you come to a future word you do not understand. Good readers, when faced with an unfamiliar word, become aggressive. They become active, not passive. They attack, and looking at the prefix, root, and suffix is one strategy good readers do."

This seems a reasonable balance to me. In five minutes, I introduced a strategy that good readers do when reading gets hard and gave my students an opportunity to practice it. As the year progresses, we occasionally (maybe once a week) take out our "What Good Readers Do" charts and add to them, five minutes here, five minutes there. I am making these strategies visible to my students, and I am doing so in a way that does not drown their reading. I am not simply teaching the reading; I am teaching the reader.

This approach contrasts a bit with what I see in the many classrooms I have visited. Often, teachers take one extreme approach or the other. Either they focus so heavily on metacognitive strategies that the actual reading gets lost (and critical reading time gets drastically cut), or they ignore these strategies completely, assuming their students already know many of them. The sweet spot, however, is found somewhere in between.

Donald Graves once said, "The teacher teaches most by showing how he/she learns" (1985, 38). This is certainly true when it comes to teaching reading. What the teacher does is more important than what the teacher says, and one of the most important things we can do as teachers when our students are wrestling with academic texts is to show them those things that good readers do.

Don't Lose Sight of the 50/50 Approach

In this chapter, I have suggested that underteaching can also lead students down the road of readicide. To avoid readicide, I suggest that teachers

✖ recognize the importance of framing.
✖ understand the value of second-draft (and third-draft) reading.
✖ adopt a big chunk/little chunk philosophy.
✖ start with the guided tour, but ease students into the budget tour to find the sweet spot of instruction.

These suggestions about avoiding the perils of underteaching are really suggestions that prove valuable in reading difficult text. But allow me to close this chapter with a reminder of the 50/50 approach I discuss in Chapter 3—that half the reading I want my students to do is recreational. That means there is no framing, no second- and third-draft reading, no big chunk/little chunk approach, no guided tour, and no time examining metacognition. No stop signs whatsoever. These approaches discussed in this chapter are valuable when reading academic texts, but let's not forget in the shadow of all this testing that our primary goal is to help our students to become lifelong readers. This will not occur if they are only doing academic reading. Although my students are wrestling with *Romeo and Juliet*, they are also reading books such as Mark Haddon's *The Curious Incident of the Dog in the Night-Time* or Dave Pelzer's *A Child Called "It."* My students are always reading two books at a time: one that requires the teacher to be in the room, and one that is a high-interest, fun read. Ignoring the recreational side of reading is a recipe for readicide. Both sides of reading—the academic and the recreational—need extensive emphasis.

Ending Readicide

The call for more testing is intensifying again. A recent study by the Center on Education Policy (2008), a nonprofit research group, demonstrates that, contrary to other studies, reading scores are actually up in most states since the No Child Left Behind Act took effect in 2002. These findings were splashed across newspaper headlines across the country. Of course, what did not make the headlines were some of the findings that were buried deep inside the study. Two, in particular, should be noted:

Test scores may be rising, but that's at least partly as a result of states lowering standards to meet the law's demand that all students become proficient by 2014. Bruce Fuller, a professor of education and public policy at the University of California at Berkeley, found that schools "lower the bar and design tests that are highly sensitive to slight gains for low achieving students. Progress may be occurring, he notes, but not anywhere near the rate claimed in this report" (King 2008). This sort of statistical manipulation is reminiscent of the handling of test scores that occurred during the "Texas Miracle."

Despite "gains" students are making on standardized reading tests, let's not forget the absurdity of penalizing schools that will not meet the goal of reading proficiency for every student by 2014. Testing expert Robert Linn reminds us that it would take 166 years for all twelfth graders to reach reading "proficiency" under this plan, and that somewhere between 70 and 100 percent of all schools will, sooner or later, fail (National Center for Fair and Open Testing 2007).

Progress was more pronounced in elementary and middle schools than in high schools. This finding is not surprising at all. In *To Read or Not to Read* (National Endowment for the Arts 2007), the most comprehensive survey of American reading ever completed, researchers found a "calamitous, universal falling off of reading" that usually occurs around age thirteen and carries forward through the rest of our students' lives (National Public Radio 2007). After years of drilling and killing, worksheets, and teaching to shallow tests, the falling off is precipitous. If it is true that test scores are rising in elementary schools—and that's a big if—what long-term price are we paying for this teaching-to-the-test approach? Students may be passing more tests, but in this holy quest to raise scores, we are killing off a generation of readers.

Is it hyperbole to say that we are killing a generation of readers? Consider some of the findings found in *To Read or Not to Read* (National Public Radio 2007):

* ✖ The first generation of students raised in the midst of electronic media read less—and less well—than previous generations of students.
* ✖ Students who read less, read less well. Students who read less well, do less well in school. People who do less well in school do less well in the workplace and participate less in civic life.
* ✖ Internet reading produces shallower reading than book reading. When reading the Internet materials, there is more emphasis on reading headlines and blurbs. Deeper reading is less likely to occur.
* ✖ The reading proficiency of college graduates fell 23 percent in the past ten years.
* ✖ Less than one out of three college graduates reads at a "proficiency" level—what used to be considered a proficient high school level of reading.
* ✖ One of three high school students in the United States drops out.
* ✖ Fifty-five percent of people who read at a "below basic" level are unemployed.
* ✖ Half of the adults in this country do not read either to themselves or to their children.

There are other ominous signs on the horizon. The Institute of Education Sciences found that students who participated in the $1 billion-a-year Reading First program—a cornerstone of No Child Left Behind—have not become better readers than students who were not in the program (Gold 2008). Their comprehension scores simply were not higher. Why might that be? Grover J. Whitehurst, director of the institute, suggests that the overemphasis on teaching skills (a worksheet approach) might be to blame. "It's possible," he says, "that in implementing Reading First there is a greater emphasis on decoding skills and not enough emphasis, or perhaps not correctly structured emphasis, on reading comprehension." This overemphasis on skills, Whitehurst finds, "doesn't end up helping children read . . . it doesn't take them far enough along to have a significant impact on comprehension" (Gold 2008, A1).

And what happens when we subject students to a treatment that "doesn't end up helping children read"? We become, as *Time* magazine calls us, "Dropout Nation":

> *In today's data-happy era of accountability, testing and No Child Left Behind, here is the most astonishing statistic in the whole field of education: an increasing number of researchers are saying that nearly 1 out of 3 public high school students won't graduate . . . For Latinos and African Americans, the rate approaches an alarming 50%. Virtually no community, small or large, rural or urban, has escaped the problem.* (Thornburgh 2006)

Surely, it does not take a leap of the imagination to understand the role that readicide is playing in the creation of "Dropout Nation."

Are We Fixing the Wrong Things?

We have heard that the sky is falling before. In "Are We Fixing the Wrong Things?" Yong Zhao (2006), a professor of education and director of the U.S.-China Center for Research on Educational Excellence, reminds us of the warnings that came from *A Nation at Risk*, a report that warned we are raising a new generation of Americans that is scientifically and technologically illiterate. However, as Zhao notes:

> *More than two decades later, the United States remains a superpower, dominating the world as the most scientifically and technologically advanced nation. The core innovations that drove the global digital revolution were created in the United States; the leaders of the computer and Internet industries are from the United States. Moreover, nearly two-thirds of the 300,000 patents issues in 2002 went to Americans. In the meantime, the countries that spurred the alarm, Japan and South Korea, have been in an economic recession for more than a decade.* (2006, 28)

How could a nation at risk—a nation of "scientifically and technologically illiterate" Americans—accomplish this? Zhao discounts the notion that it may primarily be due to importing foreign students (citing very low percentages of foreign-born students in these fields). So the question remains: how can Americans still be leading these fields when we consistently score lower in math and science than other countries? Zhao cites our "secret weapon"—"the creative, risk-taking, can-do spirit of its people." This spirit, he adds, "is not normally measured in standardized tests or compared in international studies" (2006, 31). Historically, there has been much more emphasis in developing creative thinkers in the United States, students who have been frequently encouraged to think outside the box. Our international edge has come from the cultivation of this creativity.

Unfortunately, this secret weapon, our single remaining advantage, is seriously eroding. Zhao warns that this emphasis on "centralized curriculum, standardized testing, accountability, required courses of study—could kill creativity, the United States' real competitive edge" (2006, 30). Our competitors, he notes, have already figured this out. "Whereas U.S. schools are now encouraged, even forced, to chase after test scores, China, Singapore, South Korea, and Japan—all named as major competitors—have started education reforms aimed at fostering more creativity and innovative thinking among their citizens" (2006, 30). The Chinese government, recognizing how standardized testing smothers creative thinking, has issued an executive order to minimize the consequences of testing.

Education in the United States, however, is traveling in the opposite direction. One recent study tracked 1,000 American schoolchildren from birth who enrolled in more than 2,500 classrooms in more than 1,000 elementary schools and 400 school districts (Pianta et al. 2007). Their findings warn of the United States losing its creative edge:

✖ "The average fifth graders received five times as much instruction in basic skills as instruction focused on problem solving or reasoning" (1795).
✖ The ratio of skill instruction to creative thinking (10:1) was worse in first and third grades (1795).
✖ Poor children were "highly unlikely (only 10%)" to experience classrooms with "high instructional climate across multiple grades" (1796).

The study's conclusion? Because of our nation's testing mania, students are suffering under "instruction that is overly thin and broad" (Pianta et al. 2007, 1796). Our edge—our creativity—is slipping away. While our competitors are making concerted efforts to expand the thinking of their students, American educational reform is mandating thinner and broader thinking. We are intentionally surrendering our "secret weapon," and in doing so, we are killing readers along the way. As Dana Gioia, chair of the National Endowment for the Arts, says, "The drop off in reading is now one of the most serious social and economic issues in the United States" (National Public Radio 2007). Consider these other findings found in *Reading Next* (Alliance for Excellent Education 2004):

✖ Between 1996 and 2006, the average literacy required for all occupations rose by 14 percent (8).

✖ The twenty-five fastest-growing professions have far greater literacy demands, while the twenty-five fastest-declining professions have lower than average literacy demands (8).

✖ Both dropouts and high school graduates "are demonstrating significantly worse reading skills than they did ten years ago" (8).

This downward reading trend, Gioia adds, "has enormous economic and political consequences" (National Public Radio 2007). Forcing our children through a narrower and broader curriculum is the real threat to our nation's competitive future.

Ending Readicide

So where does this leave us? What can we do to stem the tide of readicide? In considering which practices to use in the classroom, we might look at what is happening in Finland, which finished first in a recent international reading study of fifty-seven countries. By the ninth grade, Finnish teenagers (who, like American teenagers, are also obsessed with their cell phones, rap music, and electronic media) are ahead in math, in science, and in reading scores. Some features of Finnish education and culture may surprise you (Gamerman 2008):

✖ Parents of newborns receive government-paid packs of child-development materials that include books. Some libraries are attached to shopping malls. Book buses travel to remote towns so that everyone has access to books.

✖ Children do not start school until age seven.

✖ Finnish students rarely do more than a half-hour of homework a night.

✖ There are no classes for the gifted. Much more emphasis is paid to those students who are behind grade level in reading.

✖ Finnish teachers have more freedom to design lessons to meet the needs of their students. One principal says, "In most countries, education feels like a car factory. In Finland, the teachers are entrepreneurs" (Gamerman 2008, 2).

The most striking difference, however, is that in Finland there is very little standardized testing. Instead of bubbling answer sheets, students are asked to demonstrate their thinking through written and oral responses. This difference between the American approach and the Finnish approach is illustrated by a Finnish student, Elina Lamponen, who left Finland to spend a year in a high school in Michigan. She was surprised to find that the tests here were mostly multiple choice and often found herself tending to high school projects that were largely "glue this to a poster for an hour" (Gamerman 2008, 2).

I understand that the United States is not Finland and that as teachers in this country we face additional obstacles. Finland, for example, is much more culturally and linguistically homogeneous than the United States, whereas 8 percent of our student population is learning English. But it would be a mistake to completely discount the accomplishments of the Finnish on an "apples versus oranges" basis. Finland scored higher than *every* other country, including those countries that also served culturally and linguistically similar students ("apples versus apples"). How did the Finns build the best readers in the world? By eliminating standardized testing and emphasizing the importance of reading and critical thinking, by nurturing deeper thinking and creativity, and by leading their students away from the drill-and-kill instructional approach that is currently permeating American schools.

Finding Our Courage

Recently I heard Regie Routman, noted educator and author, speak at a literacy conference. She lamented the state of reading in our country and addressed the role that language arts teachers have played in this slide. "We have lost our courage," she said. "We have lost our way." She is right. We are killing readers, and in doing so, we are moving students farther away from those skills that "expert citizens" need to lead productive lives: creativity, common sense, wisdom, ethics, dedication, honesty, teamwork, hard work, how to win and lose, fair play, and lifelong learning (Sternberg 2007/2008). Worse, in the name of raising test scores, teachers and administrators actually encourage this movement in the wrong direction.

The good news is that we can find our way again. There are proven, concrete steps teachers can and must take to nurture young readers. If we are to take our students off the road to readicide, we must begin implementing key elements of the 50/50 approach:

Ending Readicide: The 50/50 Approach

In developing recreational *readers*, teachers must . . .	In developing academic *readers*, teachers must . . .
✖ never lose sight that our highest priority is to raise students who become lifelong readers. What our students read in school is important; what they read the rest of their lives is more important.	✖ teach less material and teach it deeply.
	✖ keep students' focus on the value that classic books have to offer. Illuminate the "imaginative rehearsals." Stop focusing on whether students like the books.
✖ recognize that massive test preparation is not a justification for killing readers.	✖ replace multiple-choice tests in favor of essays and other responses that require deeper thinking. Remember: what you test is what you get.
✖ always keep the 50/50 Approach in mind. Do not allow recreational reading to be drowned in a tsunami of academic reading. Maintain a balance between the kinds of reading your students do. Place a higher value on fun reading.	✖ recognize that "facts" change. Instead of memorizing them, teachers should spend more time teaching students how to think. Students need to do much more analysis, synthesis, and evaluation.
✖ provide adequate time in school to read so that students have an opportunity to develop recreational reading habits.	✖ demand that students continue to read books that may be a shade too hard for them. This is why the teacher is in the room.
✖ make sure students have access to a book flood, a place on campus where they are surrounded by high-interest reading materials.	✖ understand the cognitive development that comes when students wrestle with long books.
✖ model the importance of reading to students by being readers themselves.	✖ recognize when overteaching is occurring. Stop chopping the book up into so many pieces that the book itself gets lost.
✖ encourage students to recognize, to seek, and to maintain reading flow.	✖ recognize when underteaching is occurring and what the teacher can do to help the students get back and remain on track.
✖ stop chopping up recreational books with worksheets and quizzes.	✖ start with a guided tour, but try to set students on the budget tour as soon as possible.
✖ stop grading recreational reading. Teachers should give kids credit for recreational reading, but stop grading it.	✖ surround academic text with high-interest, authentic real-world reading.
✖ understand that recreational reading actually is test preparation. When students read books recreationally they are building valuable knowledge capital that will help them in future reading.	✖ design lessons that help students transfer the kind of thinking they are doing in the book to the kind of thinking we want them to exhibit in the real world. Help them to uncover the value found in the book.

If we are to find our way again—if students are to become avid readers again—we, as language arts teachers, must find our courage to recognize the difference between the political worlds and the authentic worlds in which we teach, to swim against those current educational practices that are killing young readers, and to step up and do what is right for our students.

We need to find this courage. Today. Nothing less than a generation of readers hangs in the balance.

IOI Books My Reluctant Readers Love to Read

Note: This list augments the lists found in my first book, *Reading Reasons*.

Coming of Age/Peer Pressure/Relationships

1. The Bluford series, Paul Langan. Life in an inner-city school.
2. *The Book Thief*, Markus Zusak. Death narrates this story of a young girl who finds solace in books during the Holocaust.
3. *Cut*, Patricia McCormick. Callie, a fifteen-year-old, is a "cutter" who seeks help for her self-destruction.
4. *Dark Angel*, Davis Klass. A family has a dark secret that is about to reemerge.
5. *Dreamland*, Sarah Dessen. This book explores the consequences of having an abusive boyfriend.
6. *Evolution, Me, and Other Freaks of Nature*, Robin Brande. Mena knew her first day of high school would be bad, but this bad? Examines the evolution debate in high school.
7. *The First Part Last*, Angela Johnson. A sixteen-year-old father struggles to care for his baby.
8. Gossip Girl series, Cecily von Ziegesar. Life inside a New York City jet-set private school.
9. *I Am the Messenger*, Markus Zusak. A botched bank robbery changes a nineteen-year-old's life.

10. *I Love You, Beth Cooper*, Larry Doyle. Denis's life changes when he blurts out in his graduation speech that he loves Beth Cooper.

11. *Invisible*, Pete Hautman. Doug, 17, has to come to terms with a tragic past.

12. *It's Kind of a Funny Story*, Ned Vizzini. A teen seeks counseling in a psychiatric hospital.

13. *Just Listen*, Sarah Dessen. An incident at a high school party has far-reaching consequences.

14. *The Kite Runner*, Khaled Hosseini. Two young boys in 1970s Afghanistan take very different paths.

15. *Lemonade Mouth*, Mark Peter Hughes. Five outcasts in detention form a bond.

16. *Looking for Alaska*, John Green. Miles, 16, is an outcast sent to a boarding school.

17. *Madapple*, Christina Meldrum. A girl raised in isolation must learn to cope with the world after her mother dies.

18. *Memoirs of a Teenage Amnesiac*, Gabrielle Zevin. A teenager loses her memory after a bad fall.

19. *My Sister's Keeper*, Jodi Picoult. Examines the difficult choices a family must make when one of the children is diagnosed with a life-threatening illness.

20. *Nineteen Minutes*, Jodi Picoult. Another delicate topic: the consequences of a high school shooting.

21. *The Pact*, Jodi Picoult. A teenage suicide has devastating consequences for two families.

22. *The Perks of Being a Wallflower*, Stephen Chbosky. Charlie, a freshman, tries to find his way in a high school.

23. *Rooftop*, Paul Volponi. A shooting becomes a focal point for social justice.

24. *The Rules of Survival*, Nancy Werlin. The story of three siblings struggling to overcome child abuse.

25. *Running Out of Time*, Margaret Peterson Haddix. Jessica, who thinks it is 1840, is more than surprised to find out it is really 2006.

26. *The Skin I'm In*, Sharon Flake. An adolescent navigates an inner-city school.

27. *Sleeping Freshmen Never Lie*, Davis Lubar. Scott Hudson hopes to survive his freshman year.

28. *Snitch*, Allison van Diepen. A teen tries to navigate between rival gangs.

29. *Someday This Pain Will Be Useful to You*, Peter Cameron. James, 18, is trying to find his way in the world after high school graduation. For mature readers.

30. *Someone Like You*, Sarah Dessen. Two best friends lean on each other when a calamity occurs.

31. *A Step from Heaven*, An Na. The trials and tribulations of a Korean family's journey to America.

32. *Strays*, Ron Koertge. Ted's parents are killed in a car crash, and his troubles are just beginning.
33. *Street Pharm*, Allison van Diepen. A teenager takes over his father's drug dealing business but must decide if it's worth it.
34. *That Summer*, Sarah Dessen. A teenage girl deals with her parent's divorce.
35. *Thirteen Reasons Why*, Jay Asher. A teenager receives haunting audiotapes after a suicide.
36. *This Lullaby*, Sarah Dessen. A modern-day teen romance.
37. *The Truth About Forever*, Sarah Dessen. A teen has to cope with her father's death.
38. *Twisted*, Laurie Halse Anderson. Tyler, busted for tagging, tries to find his way through his senior year.
39. *Tyrell*, Coe Booth. Tyrell is determined to stay clean despite a father in jail and a mother who is involved in welfare fraud.
40. *Upstate*, Kalisha Buckhanon. Two lovers are separated by a horrendous crime.

Fantasy/Science Fiction/Vampire

41. The Alfred Kropp series, Rick Yancey. Fifteen-year-old Alfred has series of adventures after finding a magic sword.
42. *A Certain Slant of Light*, Laura Whitcomb. Helen died 130 years ago, but she's still around.
43. Cirque du Freak series, Darren Shan. There is more to a traveling freak show than meets the eye.
44. The Demonata series, Darren Shan. Lord Loss, a murderous demon, is on a rampage.
45. Den of Shadows series, Amelia Atwater-Rhodes. The adventures of a 300-year-old night stalker.
46. *Elsewhere*, Gabrielle Zevin. Liz is getting younger, not older, every day.
47. The Gemma Doyle trilogy, Libba Bray. Gemma, who has visions, travels to other worlds.
48. *A Great and Terrible Beauty*, Libba Bray. *The School Library Journal* calls this novel "an interesting combination of fantasy, light horror, and historical fiction, with a dash of romance thrown in for good measure."
49. *The Host*, Stephenie Meyer. The human race is infiltrated by a species of parasites.
50. *House of the Scorpion*, Nancy Farmer. In the future, a scientist brings a number of clones to life.
51. *How I Live Now*, Meg Rosoff. A world war breaks out in the twenty-first century.
52. *Life as We Knew It*, Susan Beth Pfeffer. A meteor collides with the moon, with disastrous results for Earthlings.

53. *Mother's Helper*, A. Bates. A most unusual babysitting experience.
54. *Rash*, Pete Hautman. Life in 2076 is not easy.
55. *Rebel Angels*, Libba Bray. A sequel to *A Great and Terrible Beauty* (see above).
56. *Remember Me*, Christopher Pike. Shari is dead, and she is determined to find out who killed her.
57. The Twilight Saga series, Stephenie Meyer. A teenage romance with a vampire twist.
58. The Uglies series, Scott Westerfeld. Life in a futuristic society where everyone is "ugly."
59. *Walk of the Spirits*, Richie Tankersley Cusick. Seventeen-year-old Miranda hears voices at night.
60. Wheel of Time series, Robert Jordan. The world has been broken by a phenomenal power in this series that is reminiscent of J. R. R. Tolkien.
61. *World War Z: An Oral History of the Zombie War*, Max Brooks. The world is threatened by a zombie invasion.

Memoir and Nonfiction
62. *Always Running: La Vida Loca: Gang Days in L.A.*, Luis Rodriguez. Memoirs of an East L.A. gang member
63. *Come Back: A Mother and Daughter Journey to Hell and Back*, Claire and Mia Fontaine. A riveting account of a mother's fight to rescue her daughter from drugs.
64. *Getting Away with Murder*, Chris Crowe. The story of Emmett Till, a fourteen-year-old African American boy murdered for "inappropriately" talking to a white woman.
65. *Girl, Interrupted*, Susanna Kaysen. A sixteen-year-old is hospitalized in a psychiatric hospital.
66. *The Glass Castle*, Jeanette Walls. Another account of growing up in an eccentric, dysfunctional family.
67. *Kick Me: Adventures in Adolescence*, Paul Feig. A series of stories about the rigors of high school survival.
68. *A Long Way Home: Memoirs of a Boy Soldier*, Ishmael Beah. A twelve-year-old's account of surviving civil war in Sierra Leone.
69. *Monster: The Autobiography of an L.A. Gang Member*, Sanyika Shakur. The personal account of an L.A. gangbanger.
70. *Phineas Gage: A Gruesome but True Story About Brain Science*, John Fleischman. The incredible story of a recovery from severe trauma, and what it taught the scientific community.

71. *Running with Scissors*, Augusten Burroughs. An account of growing up in an eccentric, dysfunctional family.
72. *True Notebooks*, Mark Salzman. The author tries to reach convicts through the formation of a writing group.
73. *Undaunted Courage*, Stephen Ambrose. Meriwether Lewis overcomes disease, starvation, hostile Native Americans, and an unforgiving environment as he explores the American West.
74. *U.S. Army Survival Handbook*, Department of the Army. How to survive under the most adverse conditions.
75. *Young Men and Fire*, Norman Maclean. The courageous story of Forest Service smoke jumpers.

Poetry

76. *Burned*, Ellen Hopkins. Growing up in an abusive household, told in verse.
77. *Crank*, Ellen Hopkins. A teenager's struggle with crystal meth, told in poetic form.
78. *Glass*, Ellen Hopkins. This picks up *Crank* a year later.
79. *Paint Me Like I Am: Teen Poems from WritersCorps*, Bill Aquado. Poems written by disadvantaged youth.
80. *A Rose That Grew from Concrete*, Tupac Shakur. The poetry of the late rapper.
81. *Tears for Water*, Alicia Keys. Poems that recall the singer's childhood.
82. *Things I Have to Tell You: Poems and Writings by Teenage Girls*, Betsy Franco Yas. Teens from around the country submit poems about growing up.
83. *You Hear Me? Poems and Writing by Teenage Boys*, Betsy Franco Yas. Real-world topics addressed through poems and notes.

Sports

84. *Ball Don't Lie*, Matt De La Pena. Sticky, 17, is determined to make it out of the neighborhood through basketball.
85. *Black and White*, Paul Volponi. Two boys, "Black" and "White" try to make it to big-time basketball.
86. *Crackback*, John Coy. The trials and tribulations of teenage life, woven through the lens of a high school football team.
87. *Gym Candy*, Carl Deuker. Mick Johnson, high school football star, considers using steroids.
88. *Knights of the Hill Country*, Tim Tharp. Readers who liked *Friday Night Lights* will like this football drama.
89. *Three Days in August*, Buzz Bissinger. An in-depth, behind-the-scenes look at a three-game series between the Chicago Cubs and the St. Louis Cardinals.

Mystery

90. *Crazy Little Things*, Adam P. Knave. Twelve very strange tales.
91. *The Curious Incident of the Dog in the Night-Time*, Mark Haddon. A poodle, Wellington, has been murdered. Christopher, who is autistic, is on the case.
92. *Fake ID*, Walter Sorrells. Chase, 16, only has six days to figure out why his mother disappeared.
93. *Falling*, Christopher Pike. FBI agent Kelly Feinman is on the trail of the "Acid Killer."
94. *The Lovely Bones*, Alice Sebold. Susie Salmon recalls her murder from heaven.
95. *The Perfect Shot*, Elaine Marie Alphin. A triple homicide is not what it seems.

Graphic Novels

96. *300*, Frank Miller. Only a few hundred warriors stand against a huge army.
97. *Batman: The Dark Knight Returns*, Frank Miller. Gotham is falling apart, and Batman has not been seen for ten years.
98. *The League of Extraordinary Gentlemen*, Alan Moore. A group of adventurers are pulled together to protect the Empire.
99. *Sin City: The Hard Goodbye*, Frank Miller. Tough-guy Marv hunts the back streets to find the murderer of his girlfriend.
100. *V Is for Vendetta*, Alan Moore. Rebellion under an authoritarian British government.
101. *Watchmen*, Alan Moore. *Time* calls this story of Crimebusters a "masterpiece."

Book-of-the-Month

Name: _____

Period: _____

Book-of-the-Month

Month:

_____

Title _____

Author _____

Date started/date completed _____

Pages read _____

Rating of book (1–10) _____

Briefly summarize the book (use back side if necessary):

Author's purpose:

Intended audience(s):

Academic honesty

By signing below, I am indicating that the information on this page is accurate.

_____

Readicide: How Schools Are Killing Reading and What You Can Do About It by Kelly Gallagher. Copyright © 2009. Stenhouse Publishers.

One-Pagers

Name: _____

Period:_____

One-Pager

Title _____

Author _____

Date started/date completed _____

Pages read _____

Rating of book (1–10) _____

Choose five (5) of the following sentence starters and write a brief reflection for each. Attach your reflections to this sheet:

> I noticed . . .
> I wonder . . .
> I was reminded of . . .
> I think . . .
> I'm surprised that . . .
> I'd like to know . . .
> I realized . . .
> If I were . . .
> The central issue(s) is (are) . . .
> One consequence of _____ could be . . .
> If _____, then . . .
> I'm not sure . . .
> Although it seems . . .

Author's purpose:

Intended audience(s):

Academic honesty

By signing below, I am indicating that the information on this page is accurate:

_____

127

Name: _____

Period: _____

One-Pager

Title _____

Author _____

Date started/date completed _____

Pages read _____

Rating of book (1–10) _____

Describe the character/person who changed the most from the beginning of the book to the end of the book. Explain the change and what caused it (use back side if necessary).

Author's purpose:

Intended audience(s):

Academic honesty

By signing below, I am indicating that the information on this page is accurate:

Name: _____

Period: _____

One-Pager

_____

Title _____

Author _____

Date started/date completed _____

Pages read _____

Rating of book (1–10) _____

Describe a minor character/person in the book who had major importance. Explain.

Author's purpose:

Intended audience(s):

Academic honesty

_____

By signing below, I am indicating that the information on this page is accurate:

_____

Name: _____

Period: _____

_____ **One-Pager** _____

Title _____

Author _____

Date started/date completed _____

Pages read _____

Rating of book (1–10) _____

Describe one major external conflict and one major internal conflict found in this book (use back side if necessary):

Author's purpose:

Intended audience(s):

_____ **Academic honesty** _____

By signing below, I am indicating that the information on this page is accurate:

_____

Name: _____

Period:_____

One-Pager

Title _____

Author _____

Date started/date completed _____

Pages read _____

Rating of book (1–10) _____

Above you rated this book. Explain in detail why you gave this book that score (use the back side if necessary):

Author's purpose:

Intended audience(s):

Academic honesty

By signing below, I am indicating that the information on this page is accurate:

_____

Name: _____

Period: _____

One-Pager
_____

Title _____

Author _____

Date started/date completed _____

Pages read _____

Rating of book (1–10) _____

Evaluate the ending of the book. Considering how the book unfolded, is it an effective ending? Why? Why not? (Use the back side of this paper if necessary.)

Author's purpose:

Intended audience(s):

Academic honesty
_____

By signing below, I am indicating that the information on this page is accurate:

_____

Name: _____

Period: _____

One-Pager

Title _____

Author _____

Date started/date completed _____

Pages read _____

Rating of book (1–10) _____

If this book had gone one more chapter, what would have happened? Explain (use the back side if necessary):

Author's purpose:

Intended audience(s):

Academic honesty

By signing below, I am indicating that the information on this page is accurate:

_____

Name: _____

Period: _____

One-Pager
_____

Title _____

Author _____

Date started/date completed _____

Pages read _____

Rating of book (1–10) _____

Describe one "imaginative rehearsal" that a modern reader might take from this book. Explain how that lesson is developed (use the back side if necessary):

Author's purpose:

Intended audience(s):

Academic honesty
_____

By signing below, I am indicating that the information on this page is accurate:

_____

Readicide: How Schools Are Killing Reading and What You Can Do About It by Kelly Gallagher. Copyright © 2009. Stenhouse Publishers.

Hard Talk Checklist

Is Your School on the Road to Readicide?

Yes	No	Not Sure	
			Our school "values" reading. Do we all agree what this means?
			Is our quest for higher test scores harming our students' long-term reading prospects?
			Is it true that as our students progress from grade to grade their dislike of reading intensifies?
			Is our treatment of struggling readers helping to lift them out of the remedial reading track?
			Are the same students mired in remedial classes year after year?
			Are remedial readers even farther behind when they leave high school than they were when they entered high school?
			Is the percentage of our students who love reading dwindling?
			Are our students reading enough academic material?
			Are our students reading enough recreational material?
			Is width (coverage) drowning depth?
			Are our students being trained to think deeply?
			Are we giving our students the kinds of reading experiences that lead them to be "expert citizens"? (See page 13.)
			Does our staff understand that intensive test focus on state tests has not translated to deeper reading on other assessments, such as the SAT or NAEP assessments?
			Does our staff understand that since NCLB began, reading scores have remained flat, the achievement gap has remained wide, and fewer students today are reading?
			Does our staff understand the evidence that indicates intense testing focus actually decreases our students' college readiness?
			Does our staff understand that the end goal of this testing madness—every student will be proficient by 2014—is unattainable and is used as a hammer to push more students into a readicide curriculum?
			Are we out of balance (teaching for authentic purposes vs. teaching for political purposes)?
			Would you want your own children to be enrolled in a school that heavily emphasizes test preparation?
			Is our school/district stuck in the vicious cycle of the Paige Paradox? (See page 14.)

Alliance for Excellent Education. 2004. *Reading Next: A Vision for Action and Research in Middle and High School Literacy.* Available online at http://www.all4ed.org/files/archive/publications/ReadingNext/ReadingNext.pdf.

———. 2007. "Federal Support for Adolescent Literacy: A Solid Investment." Available online at http://www.all4ed.org/files/archive/publications/FedAdLit.pdf.

Anderson, Richard C., Paul T. Wilson, and Linda G. Fielding. 1998. "Growth in Reading and How Children Spend Their Time Outside of School." *Reading Research Quarterly* 23: 285–303.

Atwell, Nancie. 1998. *In the Middle: New Understandings About Writing, Reading, and Learning.* 2nd ed. Portsmouth, NH: Heinemann.

———. 2007. *The Reading Zone: How to Help Kids Become Skilled, Passionate, Habitual, Critical Readers.* New York: Scholastic.

Benton, Joshua, and Holly K. Hacker. 2005. "Celebrated School Accused of Cheating: TAKS Results Too Good to Be True at Houston Elementaries." *Dallas Morning News.* Available online at http://www.dallasnews.com/sharedcontent/dws/news/longterm/stories/123104dnmetcheating.add1e.html.

Burke, Kenneth. 1968. "Psychology and Form." In *Counter-Statement.* 2nd ed. Berkeley: University of California Press.

Center on Education Policy. 2008. *Has Student Achievement Increased Since 2002? State Test Scores Through 2006–2007.* Washington, DC: Center on Education Policy.

Chenowith, Karin. 2001. "Keeping Score: Competitive Reading Programs May Not Teach Kids to Love Reading." *School Library Journal,* September 1.

Ciborowski, Jean. 1992. *Textbooks and the Students Who Can't Read Them.* Boston: Brookline Books.

Collins, Billy. 1996. "Introduction to Poetry." In *The Apple That Astonished Paris.* Fayetteville: University of Arkansas Press.

Csikszentmihalyi, Mihaly. 1990. *Flow: The Psychology of Optimal Experience.* New York: Harper Perennial.

Daniels, Harvey. 2002. *Literature Circles: Voice and Choice in Book Clubs and Reading Groups.* 2nd ed. Portland, ME: Stenhouse.

EdResearch.info. "Reading by Children." Available online at http://edresearch. info/by_children.asp.

Education Trust. 2005. *Gaining Traction, Gaining Ground: How Some High Schools Accelerate Learning For Struggling Students.* Available online at http://www2.edtrust.org/NR/rdonlyres/6226B581-83C3-4447-9CE7-31C5694B9EF6/0/GainingTractionGainingGround.pdf.

Elley, Warrick. 1991. "Acquiring Literacy in a Second Language: The Effect of Book-Based Programs." *Language Learning* 41 (3): 375–411.

Epstein, Joel. 1985. "The Noblest Distraction." In *Plausible Prejudices: Essays on American Writing.* London: Norton.

Fontaine, Claire, and Mia Fontaine. 2006. *Come Back: A Mother and Daughter's Journey Through Hell and Back.* New York: Harper Perennial.

Gallagher, Kelly. 2003. *Reading Reasons: Motivational Mini-Lessons for Middle and High School.* Portland, ME: Stenhouse.

———. 2004. *Deeper Reading: Comprehending Challenging Texts: 4–12.* Portland, ME: Stenhouse.

Gamerman, Lisa. 2008. "What Makes Finnish Kids So Smart?" *Wall Street Journal,* February 29, W1. Available online at http://online.wsj.com/ public/article/SB120425355065601997-7Bp8YFw7Yy1n9bdKtVyP7KBAcJA_20080330.html.

Gladwell, Malcolm. 2005. *Blink: The Power of Thinking Without Thinking.* New York: Back Bay Books.

Gold, Maria. 2008. "Study Questions 'No Child' Act's Reading Plan: Lauded Program Fails to Improve Tests Scores." *Washington Post,* May 2, A01. Available online at http://www.washingtonpost.com/wp-dyn/content/ article/2008/05/01/AR2008050101399.html.

Graves, Donald. 1985. "All Children Can Write. *Learning Disabilities Focus* 1 (1): 36–43.

Greaney, Vincent, and Margaret Clarke. 1975. "A Longitudinal Study of the Effects of Two Reading Methods on Leisure-Time Reading Habits." In *Reading: What of the Future?* ed. D. Moyle, 107–114. London: United Kingdom Reading Association.

Haney, Walt. 2000. "The Myth of the Texas Miracle in Education." *Education Policy Analysis Archives* 8 (41). Available online at http://www.epaa.asu.edu/epaa/v8n41/.

Haycock, Kati. 1998. "Good Teaching Matters: How Well-Qualified Teachers Can Close the Gap." In *Thinking K–16*. Vol. 3, no. 2. Washington, DC: The Education Trust. Available online at http://www2.edtrust.org/EdTrust/Product+Catalog/main.htm#tq.

Healy, Jane M. 1990. *Endangered Minds: Why Children Don't Think—and What We Can Do About It.* New York: Touchstone.

Hirsch, E. D. 2006. *The Knowledge Deficit: Closing the Shocking Education Gap for American Children.* New York: Houghton Mifflin.

Jensen, Eric. 2005. *Teaching with the Brain in Mind.* Alexandria, VA: Association for Supervision and Curriculum Development.

Kain, Patricia. 1998. *How to Do a Close Reading.* Cambridge, MA: The Writing Center at Harvard University. Available online at http://www.fas.harvard.edu/~wricntr/documents/CloseReading.html.

Kim, Jimmy. 2004. "Summer Reading and the Ethnic Achievement Gap." *Journal of Education for Students Placed at Risk* 9 (2): 169–188.

King, Ledyard. 2008. "Test Scores Are Up, but Is It No Child?" *USA Today*, June 25, 7D.

Kozol, Jonathan. 2006. *The Shame of the Nation: the Restoration of Apartheid Schooling in America.* New York: Three Rivers Press.

Krashen, Stephen. 1993a. "The Case for Free Voluntary Reading." *Canadian Modern Language Review* 50 (1): 72–82.

———. 1993b. *The Power of Reading: Insights from the Research.* Edgewood, CO: Libraries Unlimited.

———. 2000. Letter to the Editor. *Education Week*, May 10.

Langer, Judith A. 2002. *Effective Literacy Instruction: Building Successful Reading and Writing Programs.* Urbana, IL: National Council of Teachers of English.

Los Angeles Unified School District. 2007. *Literary Analysis: Developing Character. A Unit Study for Grade 10.*

Markley, Melanie. 2004. "TAAS Scores Fell: Some Say State's Focus on Basics Comes at the Expense of College Prep." *Houston Chronicle*, June 6.

Marzano, Robert J., and John S. Kendall. 1998. *Awash in a Sea of Standards.* Denver, CO: Mid-Continent Research for Education and Learning.

McGill-Franzen, Anne, and Richard Allington. 2004. "Lost Summers: Few Books and Few Opportunities to Read." Available online at http://www.readingrockets.org/article/394.

McQuillan, Jeff, et al. 2001. "If You Build It, They Will Come." In *Teaching Reading in High School English Classes,* ed. Bonnie Ericson. Urbana, IL: National Council of Teachers of English.

Meier, Deborah, Alfie Kohn, Linda Darling-Hammond, Theodore R. Sizer, and George Wood. 2004. *Many Children Left Behind: How the No Child Left Behind Act Is Damaging Our Children and Our Schools.* Boston: Beacon Press.

Merriam-Webster's Collegiate Dictionary. 2006. 11th ed. Springfield, MA: Merriam-Webster. Available online at http://www.merriam-webster.com/info/new_words.htm.

National Center for Education Statistics. 2005. *National Assessment of Educational Progress.* Washington, DC: U.S. Department of Education.

National Center for Fair and Open Testing. 2007. "Reality Testing NCLB." Available online at http://www.fairtest.org/realitytesting-nclb.

National Council of Teachers of English. 2006. *NCTE Principles of Adolescent Literacy Reform: A Policy Research Brief.* Urbana, IL: National Council of Teachers of English.

National Endowment for the Arts. 2004. *Reading at Risk: A Survey of Literary Reading in America.* Research Division Report 46. Washington, DC: Library of Congress.

———. 2007. *To Read or Not to Read: A Question of National Consequence.* Research Division Report 47. Washington, DC: National Endowment for the Arts. Available online at http://www.nea.gov/research/ToRead.pdf.

National Public Radio. 2005. *Marketplace.* Interview with Barbara Bush, September 5.

———. 2007. *Talk of the Nation.* "Study: Americans Read Less Than They Used To," November 29. Available online at http://www.npr.org/templates/story/story.php?storyId=16739654.

Olson, Carol Booth. 2006. *The Reading/Writing Connection: Strategies for Teaching and Learning in the Secondary Classroom.* Boston: Allyn and Bacon.

Pavonetti, Linda M., Kathryn M. Brimmer, and James Cipielewski. 2002/2003. "Accelerated Reader: What Are the Lasting Effects of the Reading Habits of Middle School Students Exposed to Accelerated Reader in the Elementary Grades?" *Journal of Adolescent and Adult Literacy* 46: 4.

Pianta, Robert C., Jay Belsky, Renate Houts, Fred Morrison, and the National Institute of Child Health and Human Development Early Child Care Research Network. 2007. "Teaching: Opportunities to Learn in America's Classrooms." *Science* 315 (5820): 1795–1796.

Pilgreen, Janice, and Stephen Krashen. 1993. "Sustained Silent Reading with English as a Second Language High School Students: Impact on Reading Comprehension, Reading Frequency, and Reading Enjoyment." *School Library Media Quarterly* 22 (1): 21–23.

Racial Profiling Data Collection Resource Center at Northeastern University. Available online at http://www.racialprofilinganalysis.neu.edu.

Ravitch, Diane. 2007. "Get Congress Out of the Classroom." *New York Times*, October 3. Available online at http://www.nytimes.com/2007/10/03/opinion/03ravitch.html?_r=1&oref=slogin.

60 Minutes II. 2004. "The 'Texas Miracle.'" August 25. Available online at http://www.cbsnews.com/stories/2004/01/06/60II/main591676.shtml.

Sousa, David. 2004. *How the Brain Learns to Read*. Thousand Oaks, CA: Corwin.

Sternberg, Robert. 2007/2008. "Assessing What Matters." *Educational Leadership* 65 (4): 20–26.

Stevenson, Robert Louis. 1886. *The Strange Case of Dr. Jekyll and Mr. Hyde*. Jacksonville, IL: Perma-Bound Classics.

Strauss, Valerie. 2008. "Author Works to Prevent Reading's 'Death Spiral.'" *Washington Post*, March 24, B2. Available online at http://www.washingtonpost.com/wp-dyn/content/article/2008/03/23/AR2008032301754.html?nav=rss_education.

Thornburgh, Nathan. 2006. "Dropout Nation." *Time*, April 9. Available online at http://www.time.com/time/magazine/article/0,9171,1181646,00.html.

TIMSS & PIRLS International Study Center. 2007. "PIRLS 2006" and "PIRLS 2001." http://timss.bc.edu.

Toppo, Greg. 2007. "Study Gives Teachers Barely Passing Grade in the Classroom." *USA Today*, March 30, 7A.

Trelease, Jim. 2008. *NCLB: The Texas 'Miracle' That Wasn't*. Available online at http://www.trelease-on-reading.com/nclb_mirage1.html.

U.S. Department of Justice. 2000. *A Research Guide on Racial Profiling Data and Collection Systems: Promising Practices and Lessons Learned*. Washington, DC: U.S. Department of Justice.

Vygotsky, Lev. 1978. *Mind in Society: The Development of Higher Psychological Processes*. Cambridge, MA: Harvard University Press.

Wolf, Maryanne. 2007. *Proust and the Squid: The Story and Science of the Reading Brain*. New York: HarperCollins.

Wolfe, Patricia. 2004. *Brain Matters: Translating Research into Classroom Practice.* Alexandria, VA: Association for Supervision and Curriculum Development.

Wu, Yi-Chen, and S. Jay Samuels. 2004. "How the Amount of Time Spent on Independent Reading Affects Reading Achievement: A Response to the National Reading Panel." Paper presented at the International Reading Association Conference, Reno, NV, May 2–6, 2004.

Zhao, Yong. 2006. "Are We Fixing the Wrong Things?" *Educational Leadership* 63 (8): 28–31.

Zuckerbrod, Nancy. 2007. "U.S. 4th Graders Losing Ground on Literacy." November 28. Available online at http://www.bookrags.com/news/us-4th-graders-losing-ground-on-moc/.